LONDON UNDER

LONDON UNDER

PETER ACKROYD

Chatto & Windus
LONDON

Published by Chatto & Windus 2011

2 4 6 8 10 9 7 5 3 1

First published in Great Britain in 2011 by
Chatto & Windus
Random House, 20 Vauxhall Bridge Road,
London SW1V 2SA
www.rbooks.co.uk

Addresses for companies within The Random House Group Limited can be found at:
www.randomhouse.co.uk/offices.htm

The Random House Group Limited Reg. No. 954009

A CIP catalogue record for this book
is available from the British Library.

ISBN 9780701169916

The Random House Group Limited supports The Forest Stewardship
Council (FSC), the leading international forest certification organisation. All our titles
that are printed on Greenpeace approved FSC certified paper carry the FSC logo.
Our paper procurement policy can be found at www.rbooks.co.uk/environment

Typeset by Palimpsest Book Production Limited, Falkirk, Stirlingshire
Printed and bound in Great Britain by Clays Ltd, St Ives plc

CONTENTS

Bird's-eye view of the Thames tunnel, lithograph
by Thomas Hosmer Shepherd, 1851–5

1

Darkness Visible

Tread carefully over the pavements of London for you are treading on skin, a skein of stone that covers rivers and labyrinths, tunnels and chambers, streams and caverns, pipes and cables, springs and passages, crypts and sewers, creeping things that will never see the light of day. A vast concourse of people, buried deep within the clay of the Eocene period, move beneath your feet in underground trains. Rooms and corridors have been created for the settlement of thousands of people in the event of calamity. You are also treading on the city of the past, all of its history from the prehistoric settlers to the present day packed within 24 feet of earthen fabric. The past is beneath us. It exists still as the companion of the present city. It is crowded. It has its own heat. A hundred feet beneath the ground the temperature hovers at 19° Celsius or 65° Fahrenheit. It was once a little cooler, but the heat of the electric trains has quickened it. The clay surrounding the tunnels has absorbed the warmth.

In a previous book I have explored the city above the surface; now I wish to descend and explore its depths which are no less bewildering and no less exhilarating. Like the nerves within the human body, the underworld controls the life of the surface. Our activities are governed and sustained by materials and signals that emanate from beneath the ground; a pulse, an ebb, a flow, a signal, a light, or a run of water, will affect us. It is a shadow or replica of the city; like London itself it has developed organically with its own laws of growth and change. It was said of the Victorian Londoner, wrapped in fog and darkness, that he or she would not know the difference between the two worlds. The underworld is haphazard and wayward, with many abandoned passages and vast tunnels of brick leading nowhere. Beneath Piccadilly Circus is another great circus of myriad ways. The roads that converge on the Angel, Islington, have their counterparts beneath the surface.

It is an unknown world. It is not mapped in its entirety. It cannot be seen clearly or as a whole. There are maps of gas facilities, of telecommunications, of cables and of sewers; but they are not available for public perusal. The dangers of sabotage are considered to be too great. So the underworld is doubly unknowable. It is a sequestered and forbidden zone. It must be said, too, that there is little interest in this vast underworld. To fear is added indifference. What is not seen is not respected. The majority of pedestrians do not know or care that vast caverns exist beneath their feet; as long as they can see the sky, they are content.

Yet there may be monsters. The lower depths have been the object of superstition and of legend as long as there have been men and women to wonder. The minotaur, half man and half bull, lived in a labyrinth buried beneath the palace at Knossos in Crete. A dog with three heads, Cerberus, guarded the gates of the underworld in classical myth. The Egyptian god of the underworld, Anubis, was a man with the head of a jackal. The journey under ground prompted strange transformations. Anubis was also known as 'the lord of the sacred land', with the world beneath the ground creating a spiritual as much as a material presence. The great writers of antiquity – Plato and Homer, Pliny and Herodotus – have described the underground worlds as places of dream and hallucination. Most of the great religions have created temples and shrines beneath the surface of the earth. Terror lingers in caverns and caves, where there may be subterranean rivers and fires. Sixteen thousand years ago the wandering people of Europe lived in or beside the entrances to caves; but they painted frescoes in the deeper and darker spaces of the caverns. The further downward you travel, the closer you come to the power.

Good and evil can be found side by side; enchantment and terror mingle. If the underworld can be understood as a place of fear and of danger, it can also be regarded as a place of safety. A subterranean space may be the object of attraction as well as of fear. Healing wells and places of worship lie beneath the streets. Like a mother, the lower deep may have a warm embrace. It is a haven from the outside world. It is a refuge from attack. In the darkness you cannot be seen. In the world wars of the last century it became a shelter for many thousands of people. The catacombs of Rome protected the early Christians. We can repeat the words of Mr Mole to Mr Badger from *The Wind in the Willows* (1908): 'Once well underground, you know exactly where you are. Nothing can happen to you, and nothing can get at you.' 'That's exactly what I say,' Mr Badger replies. 'There's no security, or peace and tranquillity, except underground.' There has always been a London world beneath London. The author of *Unknown London* (1919), Walter George Bell, remarked that 'I have climbed down more ladders to explore the buried town than I have toiled up City staircases.' There is more below than there is above. It is stated in one London guidebook, 'certain it is that none who knows London would deny that its treasures must be sought in its depths'.

Yet malefactors of the past were also consigned beneath the surface. The medieval prison, or compter, was essentially a hole or pit in the ground. The deeper the prisoner was taken in the Tower of London, the more vile the durance. One of the least desirable places in London is the underground prison beside Clerkenwell Green known as the House of Detention. It consists of a dank and cold series of tunnels, with small cells and other rooms ranged alongside them; the structure is cruciform in shape, and was once the basement of a larger building. Much of its brickwork dates from the late eighteenth century, and it is imbued with generations of suffering. It's arches, leading to covered chambers, are of the same date. It was used as a gaol for more than 250 years, and did not finally close until 1877. It is believed by many people to be malignant and is popularly supposed to be haunted. It is appropriate, perhaps, that the shades of the dead should still wander beneath the earth. The river Styx, moving underground between the living and the dead, still flows.

The subterranean world can be a place of fantasy, therefore, where the ordinary conditions of living are turned upside down. In the nineteenth century it was seen as a sanctuary for criminals, for smugglers, and for what were known as 'night wanderers'; the cellars and tunnels beneath the ground were described as 'hidden haunts of vice' populated by 'the wild tribes of London' or the 'City Arabs'. They were supposed to harbour a criminal 'under-world' that emerged only at night. According to John

'The Mudlark', from Henry Mayhew,
London Labour and the London Poor, 1851

Hollingshead, the author of *Underground London* (1862), the tunnels were 'black and dangerous labyrinths for the innocent stranger'.

But the underworld can also become a place of romance, where the childhood impulse to hide can be indulged to the wildest extent. The idea of secret passages, of mysterious entrances and exits, of retreat and concealment, possesses an incurable charm. Yet if we are not found, in the game of hide-and-seek, what then? What if we were left alone in the darkness, our companions gone into the light?

Underground chambers and tunnels have been formed, and found, over the centuries. There are extensive catacombs in Camden Town, beneath Camden Market, and prehistoric tunnels are to be found under Greenwich Park. A German traveller of the eighteenth century noted that 'one third of the inhabitants of London live under ground'; by which he meant that the poor dwelled in the curious basements or 'cellar dwellings' that were once so common in the city. They were entered by steps leading down from the street to a well 'which was supposed to be closed at nightfall by a flap'. The poor were thus consigned to the lowest level. The vagrants of London often lived under bridges and under arches, replicating the conditions beneath the ground.

The Adelphi arches, just south of the Strand, once offered a glimpse of an old underworld. The Adelphi itself was built in the 1770s upon a series of vaults and arches that were described as 'a reminder of the Etruscan cloaca of old Rome'. In the nineteenth century these became a haven for criminals and beggars. It was reported in the public prints that assassins were concealed 'in the dark arches', such as those that make up Lower Robert Street, exploiting the passageways, tunnels, precipitous steps, sudden turnings and high-arched doorways. Horses did not like to venture through them. Stalactites hung from their roofs. Cows were stabled there, and passed their lives in darkness.

Lower Robert Street is still forbidding; it is one of the few underground streets in London, and of course has the reputation of being haunted by a murdered prostitute. In his *Picturesque Sketches of London* (1852) Thomas Miller described the region of shadows lying between the Strand and the Thames with 'the black-browed arches that span right and left, before and behind, covering many a rood of ground on which the rain never beats, nor the sunbeams sleep, and at the entrance of which the wind only seems to howl and whine, as if afraid of venturing further into the darkness'. They were another reminder of the London depths.

The geology of London is a clue to the labyrinth beneath. The city sits upon a bed of sand, gravel, clay and chalk that make up the London Basin. Deep beneath them are the rocks of the Palaeozoic period shaped hundreds of millions of years before; no one has reached them yet. Above them lie levels of ancient materials that are known as Gault clay and upper greensand. In turn they support broad bands of chalk laid down when the site of London lay below a vast sea. Upon the chalk rests the clay. London clay is thick, viscous, and malleable; it is a greenish blue colour, but in its upper reaches it is reddish brown. It was formed more than fifty million years ago. This is the material in which the underworld of London sits. It is the material through which the tunnels of the underground railway are burrowed. The clay is compressed so heavily that all of its moisture has fled; but if the pressure is lifted it will expand and, in the words of the geologist, 'come on'. We may interpret this as 'come forth'.

Above the clay is a mixture of sand and gravel from which the springs of London rise; elevators and escalator-shafts lower passengers through this sandy medium. The glaciers of the Ice Age formed the rivers that still flow beneath the surface, and descend from the upper levels of the London region into the Thames. We inhabit an inconceivably ancient space. London is based upon clay, while Manhattan is established upon layers of hard rock known as mica-schist. That accounts for the preponderance of skyscrapers in the latter city. But may it not also help to explain the manifest differences in behaviour and attitude between their citizens?

London is slowly sinking into its clay, while Manhattan seems to rise and rise into the empyrean. So we go down to the clay and the water, the old elemental things of

London. They are the origin, and they may also be the ending. The deep groundwater of the city is rising, and 15,400,000 gallons must be pumped out each day to save the entire structure.

Certain creatures roam the underworld. Rats, and eels, and mice, and frogs, abound. The brown rat from Russia is the most abundant. The native black rat was in recent years supposed to exist in certain underground quarters, beneath Oxford Street and Canning Town, but it is now more likely to be extinct. Sigmund Freud described the rat as a 'chthonic animal', an emblem of the uncanny rather than the horrid; it is a reminder of the darkness, of all that we fear. The underground can also be seen as a representation of the human unconscious, the formless and inchoate source of our instincts and desires. It preserves the 'truth' of our identity.

It is hard to estimate the number of rats beneath the city, but urban legend that they exceed the human population can be discounted. Supersonic sound is sometimes used in the sewers, sending the vermin mad with panic so that they dash themselves against the walls. It is difficult to envisage the scene. They are in any case diminished by natural forces; if they cannot escape, they are drowned in heavy rainstorms. They are rivalled by the cockroaches that can live partly on human excrement.

The oriental or common cockroach, *Blatta orientalis*, scuttles beneath the streets of central London. It lives and thrives in a horde. Reports also sometimes circulate of white crabs existing upon the walls of underground tunnels, but that may be fantastic rumour. There have even been descriptions of scorpions, an inch long and pale yellow, on the Central Line. White atrophied creatures are often known as cavernophiles.

Stray dogs, lured by the warmth and the chance of food, come into the depths. Pigeons hop on and off the trains at convenient stations. A form of mosquito, not otherwise known in England, breeds in the tunnels with a captive population upon which to feed. The species, known as *Culex pipiens*, entered the system in the early part of the twentieth century and has been expanding ever since. A magazine, *BBC Worldlife*, reported that 'the insect has evolved so fast that the difference between the overground and underground forms is as great as if they had been separated for thousands of years'. At a deep level beneath the earth the mosquitoes have returned to their primeval origins.

The underworld is the place to which our waste and excrement are consigned. For that reason public lavatories were once placed under the ground, to be reached by a flight of downward stairs. Those who worked underground – the miner or the 'flusher' of sewers – were to be feared. They were contaminated. They were closer to the devil. Radical political groups, characteristically using terror and violence as their weapons, are still known as 'underground' movements.

When a system of underground railways was first proposed in the middle of the nineteenth century, a popular preacher declared very seriously that 'the forth-coming end of the world would be hastened by the construction of underground railways burrowing into the infernal regions and thereby disturbing the devil'. When the trains did run beneath the surface, their noise was compared by one reporter to 'the shrieking of ten thou-sand demons'.

The dead are also buried beneath the ground. So the underworld is a place that induces grief. The spaces beneath the City churches were filled to bursting by the nineteenth century, and there are reports even from the medieval period of noxious vapours issuing from beneath the surface. The plague pits of London can be found from Aldgate to Walthamstow. These are the areas where, if you dig, you may 'let the plague out'. This fear is not entirely misplaced; the bacteria of the bubonic plague have long since been eroded, but the spores of anthrax can survive for hundreds of years.

There is no darkness like the darkness under the ground. It is pitched past pitch of black. You cannot see your hand before your face. The darkness enters you, as if you do not exist any more. In nightmare, this is what happens to you after death. You are suspended in eternal night. But no night is as black as subterranean blackness. It takes away all instinct for motion, because there is nowhere to flee.

It can be a vision of hell itself. In all representations of supernatural justice, heaven is above and hell is below. The topography is as fixed as east and west for the rising and setting of the sun. Order and harmony are the properties of the lighted world. All below is shapeless, formless, void. Forgotten things, discarded things, secret things, are to be found deep below.

2

Rising Up

When Christopher Wren was digging below the remains of Old St Paul's, after the Great Fire, he found Anglo-Saxon graves lined with chalk-stone. Saxon coffins of the same material lay beside them. Beneath these vestiges of a vanished civilisation were Britons, with ivory and wooden pins showing that their shrouds had been laid in rows. Below these were Roman remains and pieces of Roman pavement. Beneath these Wren found sand and seashells. Ludgate Hill had once been under the sea.

A trackway from the Bronze Age has been found on the Isle of Dogs. Gravel streets from the Anglo-Saxon period follow the course of Maiden Lane and Shorts Gardens, Floral Street and King Street; the houses along Drury Lane were 39 feet long, 18 feet wide. The bustling life persists, but the evidence for it has gone under the ground. We are treading upon our ancestors. As soon as the original city was built above the ground it began to sink. As it descended beneath the earth ground-floor rooms were transformed into basements, and the front door became the door to the cellar; the first floor was then the street level. The oldest of these remains now lie some 26 feet beneath the surface. The whole history of the city is compressed to little less than 30 feet.

Excavation of a Roman pavement in Walbrook in 1869

When the valley of the Fleet river was being cleared in the middle of the nineteenth century the pavement of an old street was discovered at a depth of 13 feet; the paving stones had been worn smooth by the passage of traffic and by innumerable footsteps. Below this street were found piles of oak, hard and black, of which the purpose was not clear. A few feet below the oak were ancient wooden pipes, which were essentially the hollowed trunks of trees. All these layers of city history were packed so tightly together that they formed a solid mass of clay, gravel, wood and stone. Just at the level of the street, a great number of pins were scattered. Whether they were hairpins, or sewing pins, the sources do not reveal.

There have in fact been stray discoveries of under-ground London over the centuries. John Stow, in the sixteenth century, reports the discovery of the shank-bone of a 'monstrous' man who stood at a height of 10 or 12 feet. It was found within St Paul's Churchyard among other bones. It seemed to Stow, therefore, that tales about a race of giants inhabiting the earth were actual truth. It is clear that these 'gyants' bones' were in fact those of a mammoth. It is sufficient to note the fact that there were considered to be marvels buried under the ground. Coins and small statues were always being found but, according to the law of the land, 'treasure hid in the earth and found shall belong to the Crown'. In the medieval period there was little interest in what lay beneath, except as a possible home for buried treasure. The underworld was otherwise the domain of demons, and should not be touched. The first Englishmen to conduct proper archae-ological studies, John Aubrey and William Stukeley, in the seventeenth and eighteenth centuries respectively, decided to concentrate on more visible sites such as Stone-henge and Avebury. Stukeley did find evidence of Julius Caesar's camp by Old St Pancras Church, and traced the line of Roman roads through eighteenth-century London;

but that was the extent of his interest. The city was in any case expanding so rapidly, extending in all directions, that no real attention was paid to the subterranean world. In a period of exponential growth, the past does not exist.

Yet it was there. In 1832 a colossal head of the emperor Hadrian was retrieved from the Thames in which it had been buried for 1,700 years. In 1865 a gang of workmen, digging beneath the surface of Oxford Street, found a curious trap-door. They opened it and were astonished to find a flight of sixteen brick steps. They followed them and 'entered a room of considerable size'. The walls were built of red brick, with eight arches originally designed to let in the light. In the middle of the chamber was a pool or bath, about 6 feet in depth. It was half-full of water, and a spring could still be seen bubbling up. It was in all probability a Roman baptistery in which the water still flowed from a tributary of the Tyburn. Yet it was demolished to make way for new building. There was still very little interest in what lay under the ground and it was consigned to what one contemporary publication called 'the abyss of oblivion'.

When in 1867 building work was being undertaken in Bouverie Street, off Fleet Street, the crypt of an ancient Carmelite monastery was revealed. It was promptly converted into a coal cellar. In the nineteenth century the world under the ground was considered in some way to be dirty and diseased. Subsequent excavations in 1910 revealed that this crypt 'is of dressed stonework. ... Deep ribs, springing from the angles and from the centre of each side, meet in a large boss carved with a rose.' So in imagination the monastery of Whitefriars rises from the ground of Fleet Street and its environs. We may see the monks in the garden walks and hear them singing their orisons. The Cheshire Cheese tavern rests upon the northern gatehouse; a garden lane, just beyond the northern wall of the monastery, has become Wine Office Court. Part of the crypt can still be seen in Ashentree Court, off Whitefriars Street. It nudges the passer-by into the consciousness of the past, but it is not much visited. When County Hall was being built, in 1910, part of a Roman ship emerged from the black silt of the ancient river; it had been sunk by a stone cannonball at the end of the third century. Thus, in random and accidental manner, that which had been buried once more came into the light.

The archaeology of the city really only began at the beginning of the last century, with salvage work undertaken by the Guildhall Museum. Largely driven by enthusiastic diggers and antiquarians the museum housed coins and pottery vessels found in all parts of London; prehistoric objects, from stone tools to bronze weapons, were taken from the Thames and added to the collection. The

Rising Up

The Roman galley discovered during the building of County Hall, 1910

curators would visit the sites of demolition or excavation, and remove any object that seemed to be of historical value. They often purchased items from the building workers themselves and accumulated many Roman, medieval and post-medieval relics. One curator, G. F. Lawrence, found more than 1,600 objects in the first six months of his employment. The past was flowing out. In this period was found the 'Palaeolithic floor' lying beneath Stoke Newington Common; it has since been covered over and concealed by new building.

The bombing of the Second World War marks the emergence of proper archaeological investigation in the city. The bombs destroyed London's present but helped to rebuild London's past. They revealed Roman London, for example, and the extent of the great Roman wall around the city became known. As the sites of bombing were thoroughly investigated, the wall rose again. In the underground car park beneath London Wall a large section of the original Kentish ragstone and red clay tiles can still be seen; in another part of the same building the foundations of the western corner of a fort have been preserved.

A fragment of London's basilica rests in the basement of a shop in Leadenhall Market. Beneath the Guildhall lay an amphitheatre capable of holding 6,000 spectators; the wooden gateway to the arena was 16 feet wide. A great building that is likely to be a cathedral, the first Christian cathedral in England, has been revealed beneath Pepys Street by Tower Hill. Will St Paul's be found on some future date beneath the earth?

In the basement of 100 Lower Thames Street extends a complete Roman bath-house; within the debris was found a Saxon brooch, dropped by a woman when clambering over the ruins. Tiled pavements of Roman London

Rising Up

Part of a Roman wall found behind the Minories,
from Charles Knight, *London*, 1841–4

have been found at various locations. Roman curses,
inscribed on pottery and stone, have also been revealed.
A painting of a robed woman lay beneath 5 Fenchurch
Street; she may have been the decoration of a tavern. An
iron ring was found at New Fresh Wharf with the inscrip-
tion *da mihi vita* (give life to me). Four stars were also
inscribed upon it, as a sign of eternity.

Piece by piece Londinium is restored. The damp earth
has preserved it so well that from the evidence once lying
beneath the ground we may conjure up a great city with

a basilica, amphitheatre, arena and numerous public buildings; we see bath-houses and monumental statues, shrines and palaces. Sacred artefacts continue to be preserved beneath the earth, such as the monumental Screen of the Gods of which only portions have been found; it now rests within the Museum of London. It was a stone façade of some 19 feet, with the images of six gods carved on either side. Some of these images remain undiscovered beneath the earth. So the under-world still contains gods and heroes. The head of a river god, carved in oolitic limestone, was discovered beneath Great Dover Street in Southwark. A carved sphinx came out of the bowels of Fenchurch Street. Bacchus had his seat of power at Poultry, where two figurines were found. Isis ruled under Walbrook, with images of her and her family close to the Mithraeum. The Mithraeum itself – the temple dedicated to Mithras in the middle of the third century – was found 18 feet beneath Walbrook, and such was the excitement aroused by the discovery that in the autumn of 1954 80,000 people visited the site. It exemplifies the power of that which has been lost and found again. The same excitement was generated by the rediscovery of the Rose Playhouse, in Southwark, during the course of excavations in 1989.

A spot of sacred ground retains its sanctity over many centuries. When the bombs of the Second World War

The head of Mithras, found buried beneath the temple nave in 1954

had reduced St Mary-le-Bow to ruins, it was discovered that its crypt was in essence a Roman building; at a depth of 18 feet a Roman road passed what must once have been the entrance to a temple above the ground. In similar fashion it was discovered that the undercroft of All Hallows, by the Tower of London, was built of Roman brick. It also once lay above the surface, and was used as a barber's shop; a groove in the pavement indicates a supply of running water. Beneath the crypt of Southwark

Cathedral have been excavated statues of Neptune and of a hunter god; an altar has also been found. There are other forms of continuity; excavations beneath the Treasury in Whitehall uncovered the waterlogged remains of two successive timber halls dating to the ninth century.

As a result of these discoveries certain streets acquire wholly new identities. Cromwell Road in West London is the site of a Saxon community, while Creffield Road in Acton has revealed Palaeolithic settlers; in Hopton Street, Southwark, a bowl from the Bronze Age has come to light. Knightrider Street, below St Paul's, concealed walls of a great terrace that has been interpreted as the retaining wall of a circus where chariot races were held; hence the name of the street. Wooden structures of the early Iron Age have been found at Richmond Terrace in Westminster, and there is evidence of a submerged forest at Bankside. There have been surprises from the first ages of the human world. A votive object, known as the 'Dagenham Idol', was buried 8 feet under the edge of the Dagenham marshes; it had been underground for almost 4,500 years. A wooden dugout canoe, containing a flint axe and a flint scraper, was recovered from beneath the Erith marshes.

Crypts, and vaults, and burial grounds, are also part of the identity of the city. Their roots are very ancient. There are photographs, in volumes of London archaeology, in which the excavator can be seen crouched over a bent skeleton, the living implicitly copying the dead. And, in large part, the original city was built upon the bones of the dead. 'It was a solemn consideration', Charles Dickens wrote in an essay entitled 'Night Walks' (1861),

> what enormous hosts of dead belong to one old great city, and how, if they were raised while the living slept, there would not be the space of a pinpoint in all the streets and ways for the living to come out into. Not only that, but the vast armies of the dead would overflow the hills and valleys beyond the city, and would stretch away all round it, God knows how far.

From Roman London alone there issued a million corpses. The graveyard of Christ Church, Spitalfields, was opened for business in 1729 and closed in 1859; between those dates some 68,000 people were somehow buried in the straitened space. At the time of excavation in 1993 soft tissue was still preserved on some of the bodies. Fears were expressed of a miasma overwhelming the archaeologists, but they were misplaced.

The excavation of cemeteries allows us to see the dead in every sense. We learn about the social and familial groups that once inhabited the city; we understand the diseases that afflicted them, and how urban life in general affected individual health. How many of the dead were natives, and how many were immigrants? A soldier, G. Pomponius Valens, was buried beneath Kingsway while Vivius Marcianus lay beneath Ludgate Hill; Celsus, a military policeman, was beneath Blackfriars. Marcus Aurelius Eucarpus, dead at fifteen, was interred in Camomile Street. A mausoleum and temple were found beneath the ground at Southwark, overlooking a roadside cemetery; the buildings had been painted with red ochre, predating the ox-blood tiles of the London Underground stations.

Almost every London church had its own cemetery. Before 1800 there were more than 200 places of burial, most of which are now unknown and unseen. In the little burial ground on the corner of Fetter Lane and Bream's Buildings there is a stone on which is carved the name of a child, 'Samewell'. This may be construed as a Dickensian pronunciation of Samuel, as in Samivell Weller, or it may simply be the same well into which we are all drawn. Our knowledge of London is increased by the buried dead. The suicides of the city were, until 1823, buried at a particular crossroads that exists still at the junction of Grosvenor Place and Hobart Place; it may therefore be deemed to be an unlucky spot.

We may also speak of the later catacombs of London, communities of the dead buried beneath the earth in

Coffins stacked in niches in the West Norwood catacombs

serried ranks and laid out in passageways and corridors at Brompton and Norwood, Kensal Green and Highgate, Abney Park and Tower Hamlets. There are ten of them, built in the mid-nineteenth century; the Victorians put their trust in burial deep below the surface. The Victorians also created a cult of death, made up of fear and sentimentality equally; the catacombs are their temples of worship. These are not as ornate or elaborate as the great ossuary beneath the surface of Paris, nor are they as intimate and claustrophobic as the catacombs of Rome. In Rome the early Christians sheltered, against persecution, alongside their dead; this element of sacred terror is absent from the London catacombs. They also differ from those of Paris. The Parisian catacombs are urban and mythical; the London variety is suburban and practical. The buildings of Brompton or of Norwood partake neither of the maze nor of the labyrinth; they are designed on a grid pattern, with a central cross. The arched brick is familiar to anyone acquainted with Victorian architecture. The dead are laid in galleries of these brick chambers striated by damp, in individual niches or stacked in bays. In 1869 the writer of a descriptive guide to Abney Park Cemetery in Stoke Newington referred to the catacomb in that graveyard as a 'cold and stony death place. ... The chilliness is awful and repulsive.'

The architecture of the 'death place', the journey under the ground, was conceived in pagan or classical terms. Some of the catacombs adopt the pediments and avenues and obelisks of the Egyptian necropolis, while the statues and pillars and temples of Highgate are borrowed from Roman originals. In the chapel of Kensal Green Cemetery is a catafalque, a hydraulic device that lowers the dead into the catacombs below. The gateway to the underworld is seen as part antiquity and part theatre. Welcome to the lower depths.

3

Holy Water

The underworld is not always considered to be unclean. It is the source of wells and springs, of healing waters and rills of moisture slaking the thirst of London. Some of them have been in place for thousands of years. In 1841 repairs were being made to the public baths in Tabernacle Street in Finsbury; the name itself is suggestive. In the course of the work a spring was found at a depth of 14 feet, and the stream issuing from it ran through an aqueduct furnished with Roman tiles. It had been constantly in use. The date of 1502 was scratched upon the aqueduct as a sign of Tudor repairs. Tabernacle Street was blessed. In 1774 many vases and sepulchral urns from the period of Romanised Britain were found in Well Walk, Hampstead; one of these urns was large enough to hold 10 or 12 gallons of water. It is likely that pots were placed as part of a religious ceremony, after the well had been freshly cut, in order to induce the flow.

Many springs once rose in London, coming up from the gravel beds beneath the surface. Londoners therefore preferred to dwell on gravel rather than on clay; that is why the gravel beds of Chelsea and Islington and Hackney were populated much sooner than the clay districts of Notting Hill or Camden Town or St John's Wood. The river Fleet, in the vicinity of Smithfield, became known as 'the river of wells'. In the thirteenth century, according to the antiquary John Stow, 'they had in every street and lane of the city divers fair wells and fresh springs'. The Great Fire damaged or choked many of them, while in the course of the rapid growth of the city others were built upon and forgotten; the construction of the sewers marked their quietus.

Many wells were once deemed to be holy, continuing a tradition of water worship that goes back to the very beginning of human history. In the Anglo-Saxon period curses were imposed 'if any man vow or bring his offerings to any well' or 'if one holds vigils at any well'. In the course of archaeological excavation, or of building work, coins and vessels are found buried beside wells; one of the most common finds is that of the lachrymatory, or vessel for tears. Coins are still thrown into wells as a harbinger of good luck. Wishing wells, and 'wakes of the well', were ubiquitous.

In the crypt of St Martin-in-the-Fields, after recent excavation, were uncovered a well together with a place of interment that can be dated to the fourth century AD; the well itself may be a remnant of pagan worship. So the church has been hiding its origin for more than 1,500 years. It has concealed its source, all the more numinous for being buried. That is another property of the underworld. Another well was found beneath the crypt of Southwark Cathedral. A well dedicated to St Chad, the patron saint of medicinal springs, was situated close to King's Cross in what is now St Chad's Place. It was so popular that on 20 April 1772, it was reported that 'last week upwards of a thousand persons drank the waters'. They cost a shilling a gallon, or threepence per quart. At the beginning of the nineteenth century the site had become a dilapidated pleasure garden, supervised by an old woman who was known as 'the lady of the well'. She would call out to passers-by, 'Come in and be made whole!' In the pump room, where the water was drawn into a large cauldron and heated, was a portrait in oils of a chubby man with a red face; he wore a cloak with a red nightcap, and was supposed to represent St Chad himself. The whole enterprise has now gone under the earth.

Close by, on the site of the present St Pancras Station, stood Pancras Wells where cows were 'kept to accommodate ladies and gentlemen with new milk and cream and syllabubs in the greatest perfection'. But these spas slowly acquired a reputation for being 'low', the haunts of ruffians and ladies of the town. So the taint of the underworld still spread, with the people using the underground water eventually dismissed as a 'rabble' and 'scandalous company'.

The presence of holy water induced various forms of theatre and ritual in its vicinity, perhaps in memory of earlier water cults and ceremonies. The Clerks' Well and the Skinners' Well close to one another in Clerkenwell, for example, were the site of the London mystery plays in the late medieval period. The well of the clerks can still be seen, behind a glass window at the turning of Farringdon Lane into Clerkenwell Green. Some broken stone steps lead down to the well, from which many generations of pilgrims or travellers drank. 'The water', in the words of an eighteenth-century antiquarian, 'spins through the old wall. I was there and tasted the water, and found it excellent, clear and well tasted.' Close by was a spring known as Black Mary's Hole, the name believed to be a degeneration of Blessed Mary's Well; the whole process of naming is an apt token of the darkening fate of London's springs. Other derivations have been suggested. The well may have belonged to the convent of St Mary's, Clerkenwell, where the Benedictine nuns wore their familiar black habits. It may have been the property of a woman, Mary, who owned a black cow or alternatively by a black woman of the same name. It may have been dedicated to the 'black Madonna', the

Virgin depicted in the early medieval period with dark skin. The names of London are mixed and mingled, compounded by folklore and superstition. Black Mary's Hole was believed to be buried for ever, but in 1826 its wood covering disintegrated and a large hole appeared in the footpath. The neighbourhood of Islington, of which Clerkenwell is a part, was the site of many such wells. Hence the verse of a confirmed invalid who had tried the waters of various spas:

> But in vain till to Islington's waters I came
> To try if my cure would add to their fame.

St Clement's Well was known as Holy Well, giving its name to Holywell Street where pornographic literature was sold in the nineteenth century. 'It is yet faire and curbed square with hard stone,' John Stow wrote, 'and is always kept cleane for common use. It is always full and never wanteth water.' Holywell Street was demolished in 1901, as a result of the 'improvements' that led to the building of Kingsway, but the site of the well can still be located. It lies on the spot just north of the Strand beside Clement's Inn. On Holy Thursday or Maundy Thursday newly baptised converts, wearing white robes, would congregate about the well. Another holy well lies close by, now in the basement of Australia House on Aldwych, that may have confused the pilgrims.

St Bride's Church, in Fleet Street, rises above the site of St Bride's Well; the name of Bridewell of course derives from the same source. It was once one of the great spiritual centres of London, but was diminished to secular use by the end of the sixteenth century. It met its end on the occasion of the coronation of George IV, in the summer of 1821, when thirsty visitors are said to have drained it. A plane tree by the south-east corner of the church marks the spot. A holy well was located in Hyde Park, St Agnes's Well, where sick children were immersed. A square metal panel, in front of the pavilion of the Italian Gardens, is its only memorial.

Sadler's Wells was originally a well serving the monks of St John's Priory, Clerkenwell, but its name derives from a more recent date. John Sadler had in 1683 employed some workmen to dig for gravel in his garden, when one of their spades struck a flat stone supported by four oaken posts; beneath it was a large well of stone arched over and 'curiously carved'. Here was found an apparently endless supply of mild chalybeate water – water rich in iron – that until recent times could be purchased in the Sadler's Wells Theatre. It was also employed in the theatre's air-cooling system. The well itself survives. It is of some interest that the theatre or 'musick house' was established at the beginning of the eighteenth century and has continued its life ever since. In the nineteenth century it was described as the 'Aquatic Theatre' and was known for the 'real water effects' upon the stage. Other entertainments were on offer. One performer would eat a live cock, complete with feathers and innards, washed down with half a pint of brandy.

The 'musick house' at Sadler's Wells, in 1813

Much of the London water springing to the surface was impregnated with various minerals imparted by the gravel and the clay, and so as a result innumerable spas or 'spaws' were established in the eighteenth century to cure certain common ailments. A good mixture of water with iron, or magnesium sulphate, or sodium sulphate, 'strengthens the Stomach, makes gross and fat bodies lean and lean bodies fleshy'. In the words of another contemporary pamphleteer, 'this water taken internally would prevent or cure Obstructions and Tumours of the Liver, Spleen . . . also Flatus Hypochondriacus, Black and Yellow Jaundice, Scurvy and Cholerick Passion'. Chalybeate water, in particular, was a sovereign curative for those with skin diseases or diseases of the eye. Eyes and water have an affinity. That is the significance of the lachrymatory. In the nineteenth century the water was more commonly applied to mangy dogs.

An eighteenth-century street cry of London rang out with 'any fresh and fair spring water here!' Something in the atmosphere of the wells encourages the ministrations of what has become the medical profession. The houses of fashionable doctors, in Devonshire Place and Upper Wimpole Street, lie directly above the wells and gardens of Marylebone Spa. But the waters all went back into the ground. The only uncontaminated water from a London spring, at the beginning of the twentieth century, was being drawn from Streatham Well. That also has now been buried.

The names remain as a token of past time. Spa Fields, opposite Sadler's Wells, is now the site of a tower block. A public house in the immediate vicinity, the London Spa at the corner of Rosoman Street and Exmouth Market, was opened on 14 July 1685 by Robert Boyle. The eminent scientist might not have anticipated that, on the same site, a public house with the same name would stand at the beginning of the twenty-first century. In the winter of 1851 an ancient well was found beneath the yard of the Lamb public house in Lamb's Conduit Street; the well has gone but the public house survives.

Wells and springs are places of transition, where the underworld rises out of the ground. They encourage song and dance; they are the site of ritual. The plethora of London names such as Spring Gardens, Well Walk and Wells Street testifies to the extent and variety of these waters. We also have Shadwell and Stockwell and Camberwell. It would be weary work to enumerate all the buried wells of London. It is enough to know that they once existed.

4

Forgotten Streams

The thirteen rivers and brooks of London still flow. Once they passed through fields and valleys, and now they run along pipes and sewers. But they have survived through the human world. They are buried, but they are not dead.

The Westbourne rises in Hampstead and makes its way to the Thames at Chelsea. On its route it passes through Kilburn and gathers strength before flowing southwards through Paddington towards Hyde Park. It once replenished the Serpentine, and that body of water still rests in the valley it created. The knight's bridge was over the Chelsea reach of the Westbourne, giving its name to the neighbourhood. The area of Bayswater was also named after the river. Kilburn, or *cyne-berna* (royal stream), is another beneficiary.

On its journey to the Thames the Westbourne passes through a great iron pipe to be seen above the platforms of Sloane Square tube station. In the eighteenth and early nineteenth centuries it ran through desolate fields and muddy swamps, but the territory was drained and covered before being transformed into Belgravia. Eleven streets in Paddington are named after the river – among them Westbourne Grove and Westbourne Gardens – and Bourne Street in Chelsea follows its course. It is often possible to track the path of the river by contemplating the street names on the outer surface. The Westbourne is now known as the Ranelagh sewer.

The Westbourne tumbling from the Serpentine in 1800

The Effra descends from Norwood, South London, making its way through Dulwich and Herne Hill before entering Brixton; it was 6 feet in depth here, and from bank to bank measured 12 feet.

It was wide enough to support large barges, and King Canute is recorded to have sailed up the Effra to Brixton. The name itself derives from *yfrid* or torrent. At the beginning of its descent, in Norwood, there still stands an old cottage named 'The Boathouse'. On the Brixton Road small bridges connected the houses with the road itself; the grass verges on either side of the road still mark the banks of the river. The old riverscape survives. There is a Water Lane and a Coldharbour Lane and a Rush Common in Brixton. The Effra then ran past what is now the south side of the Oval before leaving Kennington and reaching Vauxhall. A stage or platform was erected, during the mid-Bronze Age, at the point where the river flows into the Thames; the place where rivers meet was deemed to be holy.

The history of the Effra is representative. Its upper parts were relatively clear and clean; in the latter part of the eighteenth century it was a swiftly running and amiable stream guarded by laburnums, hawthorns and chestnut trees. As it approached the suburbs of the city, however, it gradually became fouled until it was little more than a sewer. It was eventually covered by brick and building. There is still a small open stretch in Dulwich, and the Effra overflows into areas of Dulwich Park and Dulwich Common. Although it is largely concealed it can still flood its neighbourhood at times of heavy rain; the adjacent area was last inundated in the summer of 2007. Further downstream it can only be entered through the sewers of the Effra Road in Brixton, but there have been suggestions that parts may be opened up once more as a fitting addition to the London environment.

The Walbrook lies to the north, in the City of London, where a narrow street is still devoted to its memory. John Stow was already mourning its disappearance at the end of the sixteenth century. 'This water-course,' he wrote, 'having divers bridges, was afterwards vaulted over with brick, and paved level with the streets and lanes where through it passed; and since that, also houses have been built thereon, so that the course of Walbrooke is now hidden underground, and thereby hardly known.'

We can revive that course in the imagination. It rose in the vicinity of Holywell Street in Shoreditch, and indeed that sacred spring may be its source. There are signs of a Roman shrine at this spot. It then ran southwards towards the city on a course now marked out by Curtain Road and Blomfield Street; it passed across the wall just to the west of the church of All Hallows; an aqueduct was found here, buried at a depth of 20 feet. An arch was found at its southern end lined with moss; at some time, therefore, the channel had been above the ground.

From this point the river flowed south-west until it

reached Tokenhouse Yard, a little to the north-east of the Bank of England; it may have been enlarged by one or two small tributaries and, when it was still visible, at least four bridges were built across it. The church of St Margaret Lothbury was also erected on vaults above the flowing water. The Walbrook then turned slightly to the south-west and coursed beneath the Bank, from where it ran beneath St Mildred, Poultry. The church, now demolished, was rebuilt on an arch over the river in 1456. In 1739 the Walbrook was described as 'a great and rapid stream . . . running under St Mildred's church steeple at a depth of sixteen feet'. The Bank and the Mansion House are built upon the alluvial deposits from the river.

From St Mildred, Poultry the river ran south beside the Roman temple of Mithras that had been erected on the bank beside it. It then descended towards the Thames on a path 50 yards to the west of the present street named Walbrook, where it ran beside St Stephen upon Walbrook. It then flowed down to Cloak Lane, named after *cloaca* or sewer. The attachment of churches to the river – or of the river to churches – is confirmed by the fact that at Cloak Lane there stood another church, St John the Baptist upon Walbrook.

It then ran down Dowgate Hill towards the Thames with such force that in 1574 a young man of eighteen tried to leap across it but was carried away by 'such violent swiftness as no man could rescue or stay him till he came against a cart wheel that stood in the watergate before which he was drowned and stark dead'. These are the violent waters that now lie 35 feet under the ground. Yet they do mark the world above the ground. A sharp turn in the river's course became Elbow Lane, later changed to College Street. A dip along Cannon Street, between Budge Row and Walbrook, still signals the valley through which it passed.

So the Walbrook began at a sacred well and touched at least six holy places in the course of its journey. Another testimony to its character may be found in the discovery of skulls deposited in its waters at some point in the first century. Forty-eight human skulls were found in the bed of the river, during excavations in the middle of the nineteenth century, and more recent investigation has shown that they were deliberately immersed without their lower jaws; the colour of the bones suggests that they had been exposed after death. It is very likely, therefore, that the Walbrook was the site for ritual activity. At the time of the immersion of the skulls it was some 12 feet in width but relatively shallow. It then fell into a decline, but was rescued for use in the eleventh and twelfth centuries when it was described as 'a fair brook of sweet water'; the growth and intensification of London meant that, by the thirteenth century, it had become an open sewer full of dung and other refuse. By the sixteenth century it was largely covered. It had begun another phase of its long life.

Yet it still had its uses. It was an administrative boundary whereby according to Stow 'the procedure, according to ancient usage of the City of London, is wont to be that eighteen men must be chosen from the east side of the Walebroke, and eighteen men from the west side' for various civic duties. Stow also reports that twelve wards lay on the west side of the river, and thirteen wards on the east. In its lower reaches, for example, it divided the wards of Dowgate and Vintry. Its etymology may be *wealas*, or stream of the Britons, encouraging speculation that the Walbrook separated the native Britons from the Roman administrators. But that must remain in the realm of theory only. Other London rivers acted as the boundaries of wards or parishes, and their invisible presence still marks a difference in atmosphere between adjacent City neighbourhoods.

The Tyburn springs up in Hampstead and journeys south through Swiss Cottage and Regent's Park before it joins with a tributary and follows a meandering path into central London. The twists and turns of Marylebone Lane accurately plot its course. The primeval force of water has created these shapes, cutting its way through clay that has now become brick. Old sketches delineate the Tyburn in this part of its progress, flowing through fields with flowers and bushes beside its banks. If you look carefully enough you can still glimpse the hills and valleys of the original landscape, even though they are now covered by bricks and stone rather than trees and grass; they make up the contours of the modern city.

From Marylebone Lane the Tyburn follows a south-ward course across Oxford Street, where it then turns south-east into South Molton Lane; Brook Street is named after it. It then pursues a circuitous course through the purlieus of Mayfair before finally emerging into Down Street where naturally enough it descends into Piccadilly. Oxford Street was once known as the Tyburn Road, and Park Lane as Tyburn Lane; the river of course also gave its name to the gallows set up by Marble Arch. The name Marylebone is derived from the church of St Mary by the bourne or brook.

The Tyburn then crosses Green Park, flows past Buck-ingham Palace, and runs through Victoria and Pimlico into the Thames by Vauxhall Bridge. This was until recent times an area of marsh and swamp, so that the waters of the Tyburn in the vicinity were not much used. In *A Trav-eller's Life* (1982) Eric Newby recounts how he came upon the stream in 1963 and recalls that 'the bottom of the Tyburn was littered with some bizarre sorts of jetsam which included that morning a fine pair of unmounted antlers, a folio Bible in the Welsh language, half a pram and an old bicycle'. Rivers seem to attract unwanted and dilapidated things; consigned to the water, they can be made to disappear. The upper reaches of the Tyburn were far more wholesome, and in the thirteenth century a conduit was built to carry the water through wooden pipes from Marylebone Lane into the City. It was eventually discharged at the great conduit in Cheapside.

Other lost rivers flow north of the Thames, among them Stamford Brook that rises at Wormwood Scrubs in East Acton and falls into the Thames at Hammersmith. In its closing stages it becomes three streams, with myriad tributaries crossing and recrossing beneath the pavements unseen and unknown. Another river, Counter's Creek, finds its source somewhere beside Kensal Green cemetery before passing through White City, Olympia and Earls Court; it reaches its end at Chelsea, close to Lots Road Power Station, where in the 1950s it was noticed as 'a stagnant ditch with a few disheartened marguerite daisies and thistles growing beside the green slime'. On its route from Kensal Green Cemetery it passes close to Hammersmith Cemetery and Brompton Cemetery and Fulham Cemetery, perhaps out of atavistic attraction to the buried dead. Hackney Brook, in the east of London, also forms the northern boundary of Abney Park Cemetery. The buried river known only as the Black Ditch rose in Whitechapel.

Many people are fascinated by the course of the subterranean rivers; they track them, sometimes with maps and sometimes with dowsing rods, seeking for the life under ground. They pursue them as far as they can through unpromising surroundings of council blocks or shopping malls or derelict plots of marshy land. On stretches of their route the outer world is in mourning for its lost companion. A verse from Job may act as a summary: 'Even the waters forgotten of the foot: they are dried up, they are gone away from men.'

The river walkers pace their journey slowly, re-creating a sense of time that has been lost in the contemporary city – or perhaps time is altered by the presence of the buried river. It may follow the speed of the water beneath the ground. Time itself does not matter in the presence of the lost river. The Tyburn, for example, flowed in prehistory just as it flows now; it joins past and present in a perpetual embrace. We might be in Coleridge's 'Xanadu'

> where Alph, the sacred river, ran
> Through caverns measureless to man
> Down to a sunless sea.

The Neckinger flows south of the Thames; it has its origin beneath the Imperial War Museum, formerly Bethlem

Hospital for the insane, and then runs under Elephant and Castle before following the New Kent Road; it turns north-east into Prioress Street and Abbey Street, the site of Bermondsey Abbey. The monks built a bridge across it here. It then runs northward to the Thames. St Saviour's Dock marks the point where it issued into the greater river, where Neckinger Wharf once stood. It is said that pirates were hanged here; the rope that killed them was known as 'the devil's neck cloth' or 'neckinger'.

Its channels, in the lower reaches, formed one of the most notorious London districts. Jacob's Island was immortalised by Dickens as the home of Bill Sikes in *Oliver Twist*, and was dubbed in the *Morning Chronicle* as the 'Venice of Drains' and the 'Capital of Cholera'. It was a place of filth, rot and garbage. Jacob Street is the only memorial of that tainted past. The Neckinger has in any case always been a symptom of urban squalor. It was used by tanners and hatters in the course of their work so that it was said to resemble the colour of strong green tea. Charles Kingsley visited the neighbourhood of the river in 1849 and exclaimed to his wife, 'Oh God! What I saw! People having no water to drink – hundreds of them – but the water of the common sewer which stagnates . . .'

Underground water has often been associated with disease; it is perceived to be insidious or threatening, and therefore becomes the cause of ague and pestilence. Just as it may undermine the foundations of houses along its course, so it may break down the health of those who live by or near it. In earlier years the most common ailments were typhoid fever and cholera, but the dwellers by underground streams are now more likely to contract bronchitis or rheumatism. A survey from the last century concluded that those who live beside waterways, whether open or buried, were more likely to suffer from asthma and hay fever.

There is another interesting phenomenon associated with the lost rivers of London. In his survey entitled *The Geography of London's Ghosts* (1960), G. W. Lambert concluded that approximately three-quarters of the city's paranormal activity takes place near buried waters. Some may conclude that the spiritual properties of the rivers have been confirmed; the ritual activity at the Walbrook, for example, may thereby be justified. The more scep-tical will believe that the flowing of buried waters merely creates strange effects of sound.

Smaller underground streams can be found in the area of South London, among them the Peck and the Earl's Sluice that join forces before entering the Thames at Deptford. To the west lie the Falcon and the Wandle. The Falcon has two origins, Balham and Tooting, before they unite at Clapham; the underground stream enters the Thames at Battersea.

* * *

The Wandle, by J.B. Watson, *c.* 1819

The river Wandle is better known, and for much of its length it runs above the ground. It rises in Croydon and in its journey of 9 miles to the Thames it passes through Lambeth and Wandsworth; it helps to form the boundary between Croydon and Lambeth as well as that between Merton and Wandsworth. Wandsworth means the village by the Wandle.

It was well known for its fish. In 1586 William Camden

described it as 'the cleare rivulet Wandle, so full of the best trouts'. In *The Compleat Angler* (1653) Izaak Walton also complimented it on its trout. Lord Nelson used to fish in its waters, where they entered Lady Hamilton's garden at Merton; she renamed it 'the Nile' in his honour. It is still the haunt of fishermen; there is an organisation called the 'Wandle piscators'. John Ruskin recalled how 'the sand danced and minnows darted above the Springs of Wandel'. It is even commemorated in charming verse:

> Sweet little witch of the Wandle!
> Come to my bosom and fondle.
> I love thee sincerely,
> I'll cherish thee dearly,
> Sweet little witch of the Wandle.

One observer of the rivers in the early twentieth century, Hilda Ormsby, remarked in *London on the Thames* (1924) that the Wandle 'particularly seems to resent being buried alive'. It can be seen as a living thing, therefore, with its own character and its own energies. Yet there are some underground rivers that seem more alive, and more powerful, in their subterranean existence. We will go on a journey along the Fleet.

5

Old Man River

The most powerful of all London's buried rivers is undoubtedly the Fleet. It has its own history as complex and as varied as that of the city itself. It has created its own mythology. A number of poems have been dedicated to it. It rises at two spots on Hampstead Heath before flowing down the Fleet Road to Camden Town. Even its origin has been granted literary associations. Samuel Pickwick read a paper to the Pickwick Club, on 12 May 1827, entitled 'Speculations on the Source of the Hampstead ponds, with some observations on the Theory of Tittlebats'. At a later and more melancholy date in his illustrious career Pickwick found himself incarcerated within the Fleet Prison. So he came to know the river well.

Its name derives from the Anglo-Saxon *fleotan*, meaning to float, or from the Saxon *flod* or flood. Technically it might be taken to describe a tidal inlet. It has been known as the River of Wells, also a very accurate description. Its two sources are united north of Camden Town, where in the early nineteenth century the river was more than

60 feet wide; an anchor was found in the riverbed here, suggesting that it was possible for boats to reach upriver into what were then the outskirts of London. It ran south past Old St Pancras Church towards King's Cross. The parishioners of St Pancras complained in the fifteenth century that their church stood 'where foul ways is and great waters'. From that point forward the modern streets give a clear indication of its course.

In vision we see the slopes of the hills and valleys all around us, as we walk along King's Cross Bridge into St Chad's Place before turning right into King's Cross Road; the adjacent roads here rise up on the left hand, in an area that was once the haunt of wells, springs and pleasure gardens. As we proceed along the valley of Pakenham Street and Phoenix Place and Warner Street, the roads now rise on the right-hand side and we see Eyre Street Hill and Back Hill. This was a place of green banks and gardens, and we can still walk up Vine Hill and Herbal Hill. The river then turns southward into Farringdon Lane and Turnmill Street, where once its current turned three mills. An advertisement for a house to let in that street, in the *Daily Courant* of 1741, mentions 'a good stream and current that will turn a mill to grind hair powder or liquorish or other things'.

The river goes south-west into Cowcross Street, and flows down Saffron Hill. This is the place where the bishops of Ely cultivated saffron in the fifteenth century and, at a later date, strawberries. The river then plunges into the great valley of Farringdon Road and Farringdon Street and New Bridge Street; it eventually decants into the Thames at Blackfriars. There were two islands or 'eyots' in the lower part of its course, before it reached the larger river, testifying to a width of approximately 40 feet.

Five bridges once spanned the lower part of the Fleet, three of them stone. Holborn Bridge rose where Holborn Viaduct now stands; Holborn is a derivation from 'old bourne' or old stream. Turnagain Lane, off Farringdon Street, was a cul-de-sac that led down to the bank of the river, hence its name. To its east rose a gravel hill, on which part of the City was built, and to its west lay a marshy fen that was not completely drained. The Fleet was the western boundary of Roman London, and remained in use as a territorial line for 2,000 years. At the time of the Civil War it became the point where earthworks were erected to defend the City. It still marks the border of Westminster and the City.

It was a notable river, therefore, flowing through what would become the heart of London. A petition of 1307 states that the Fleet 'used to be wide enough to carry ten or twelve ships up to Fleet bridge, laden with various articles and merchandise'. In the twelfth century it was used for transporting stones to help in the building of

Old St Paul's. It was also employed for conveying hay, and corn, and wine, and wood. Old Seacoal Lane and Newcastle Close bear witness to another London necessity that was discharged at one of the wharves.

The confluence of the Fleet and the Thames, 1749

But the curse of the city was already upon it. The slaughter-houses of Smithfield, and the tanneries along its banks, discharged all of their waste products into the waters. It was constantly fouled almost to choking by refuse and silt, and only periodic attempts were made at cleansing. It was scoured clean at the beginning of the sixteenth century, for example, so that boats could once again sail up to Fleet Bridge and Oldbourne Bridge. It was thoroughly cleaned a hundred years later, and again in 1652 when it was clogged 'by the throwing in of offal and other garbage by butchers, saucemen, and others, and by reason of the many houses of office standing over upon it'. A 'house of office' was a public lavatory. It was now in its lower reaches a brown soup.

Ben Jonson's poem 'On the Famous Voyage' (1612), celebrates – if that is the word – a journey up the Fleet at the beginning of the seventeenth century:

> In the first iawes appear'd that ugly monster
> Yclepèd Mud, which, when their oares did once
>   stirre,
> Belched forth an aire, as hot as the muster
> Of all your night-tubs, when the carts doe cluster,
> Who shall discharge first his merd-urinous load . . .
> The sinks ran grease, and hair of measled hogs,
> The heads, boughs, entrails, and the hides of
>   dogs.

He goes on to enquire:

> How dare
> Your daintie nostrils (in so hot a season,
> When every clerke eates artichokes and peason,

Laxative lettus, and such windie meat)
Tempt such a passage? When each privies seate
Is fill'd with buttock? And the walls doe sweate
Urine and plaisters?

A hundred years later Jonathan Swift, observing the waters flowing under Holborn Bridge, remarked in 'A Description of a City Shower' (1710) that:

Sweepings from Butchers Stalls, Dung, Guts and
  Blood,
Drown'd Puppies, stinking Sprats, all drench'd in
  Mud,
Dead Cats and Turnips-Tops come tumbling
  down the Flood.

After the Great Fire of 1666 Sir Christopher Wren determined to replace the river of shit with a river of majesty. He widened the Fleet and gave it some of the characteristics of a Venetian canal, with wharves of stone on either side and with a grand new Holborn bridge. This bridge was found beneath the ground in 1826, having in the end been surmounted by the rubbish of the city. Forty years after Wren's renovation Ned Ward, in *The London Spy* (1703), remarked that 'the greatest good that I ever heard it did was to the undertaker, who is bound to acknowledge he has found better fishing in that muddy stream than ever he did in clear water'. George Farquhar, in *Sir Harry Wildair* (1701), refers to 'the dear perfume of Fleet Ditch'. Alexander Pope completes this litany of Fleet elegists with the *Dunciad* (1728), in which the river forms the suitably murky background to a satire on London corruption and wretchedness; on its stream rolls 'the large tribute of dead dogs to Thames'.

The canal was found to be less than useful to the merchants and wholesalers who, by encroaching on the whole area, reduced it to chaos and dirt once more. On 24 August 1736 the *Gentleman's Magazine* reported that 'a fatter boar was hardly ever seen than one taken up this day, coming out of the Fleet Ditch into the Thames. It proved to be a butcher's near Smithfield Bar, who had missed him five month, all which time he had been in the common sewer, and was improved in price from ten shillings to two guineas.' In the winter of 1763 a barber from Bromley, the worse for drink, fell into the waters and was so enmired in mud that he froze to death overnight.

Eventually the canal was built over, and the wharves became streets; a public market was erected just above the junction with Fleet Street, now called Ludgate Circus, and in the 1820s Farringdon Street was built. The task of hiding the Fleet was more or less complete. Yet it was not wholly or safely buried. In 1846 it blew up and its fetid gases, as well as its waters, escaped into the outer world. The roads became impassable, and the houses inundated. Three poorhouses were deluged and partly destroyed by a great wave of sewage. A steamboat was smashed against the Blackfriars Bridge. At times of storm the river still proves hazardous for those who live along its course. The tunnels of London Underground in the vicinity are kept dry by means of pumps.

The Fleet Ditch, behind Field Lane, 1841

The archaeology of the area is matter for wonder and contemplation. The skeleton of an infant was found on

59

the southern edge of one of the two islands; the child came from a time before the foundation of Roman London, but the anaerobic conditions allowed some of its flesh and skin to survive. Whether it drowned, or was killed, is of course not known. Glass kilns were built by the eastern bank of the river in the third century. Evidence also exists from the Roman period of coins and pottery, of rings and glasses, of leather shoes and wooden writing tablets, of spatulas and hooks used for surgical purposes. Three keys from the medieval period had dropped down to the Roman level. The foods of various periods – the fruits, the nuts, the cereals – have been found. All the panoply of early London life is here.

Yet time may also be suspended above the river. Traces of the Roman road leading out of Newgate have been discovered; the modern Holborn Viaduct follows precisely the same path. The same building stood on Ludgate Hill, overlooking the Fleet, from the twelfth century until a night in 1940 when it was destroyed by fire bombs; it had no doubt served a variety of purposes over its long life, including those of a shop, an inn and a lodging house.

An octagonal stone building, most likely to be a Romano-Celtic temple, was built close to the banks of the river. Its interior was red with a border of green and white lines. A pit beside it contained flecks of charcoal and a human skull. The Fleet was once a sacred place, associated with the Celtic worship of the head. The skulls of the Walbrook offer a parallel. The temple was destroyed at the beginning of the fourth century, at the time when Christianity had become the dominant religion of London. A large building of many rooms was then built on the same site. It has been suggested, therefore, that the temple was torn down and a bishop's palace erected in its place. Two Roman images, of Bacchus and of Ceres, had been flung into the waters; the *Mirror* of 22 March 1834 also reported the discovery of 'a considerable number of medals, with crosses, crucifixes and Ave Marias engraved thereon'.

At the place where the Fleet and Thames become one, eleven bodies from the early part of the eleventh century were uncovered in the early 1990s by a team of archaeologists working for the Museum of London Archaeology Service; the bodies had been dismembered and decapitated before being buried. A toilet facility of three seats, dating from the twelfth century, was found deposited in the mud as a reminder of one of the river's original functions. A black rat, the harbinger of plague, was also found.

Gazing on the maps of the Fleet and the Fleet Valley, and studying the archaeology of the area, can turn the development of London into a dream or hallucination. Buildings rise and fall, road surfaces are relined before falling into disuse, yards and alleys disappear and reappear, doorways and staircases come and go, lanes run through previously unoccupied areas, alleys become streets, wells and new drains and cellars are dug in profusion before being covered over. A dish appears bearing the picture of a Tudor woman, and an anthropomorphic head of the thirteenth century emerges from the mud. Buried in the debris of the Fleet were toys, vessels, tobacco pipes, wooden panels, brooches, pots, bowls, jugs, buckles, pins and pieces of fabric. On one tile was imprinted the fingermark of a small child. It is liquid history.

The Fleet river was always synonymous with crime and disease, not least because of the Fleet Prison that stood beside its eastern bank. This place of dread reputation is mentioned for the first time in documents of the twelfth century, and was no doubt built a few decades earlier. It was erected upon one of the two islands of the Fleet, with a bridge connecting it to the mainland of the city ditch; the 'Gaol of London', as it was called, was surrounded by a moat 10 feet in width. It consisted of a stone tower with an unknown number of floors; it may have therefore resembled the White Tower of the Tower of London. Many cups and mugs have been found in the precincts of the prison; one of them was inscribed 'J. Hirst, Fleet Cellar'. The prison stood for almost 800 years before being demolished in 1845.

A stairway to the buried Fleet

Other criminal fraternities congregated along the course of the Fleet. A house, looking over the river close to Smith-field, became in the eighteenth century a haven for thieves and footpads of every description. A trap-door in the building led directly down to the water, and the victims of crime were sometimes unceremoniously bundled out. One sailor had been decoyed before being robbed and stripped; he was 'taken up at Blackfriars bridge a corpse'. When 'the Old House in West Street', as it was known, was demolished its cellars were full of human bones. Turn-mill Street was notable for its brothels, and Saffron Hill for its robbers. In the nineteenth century William Pinks,

63

in his *History of Clerkenwell* (1881), remarked that 'vice of every kind was rampant in this locality, no measures being effectual for its suppression; the appointed officers of the law were both defied and terrified'.

The association with disease was just as strong as that with criminality. In the twelfth century the monks of Whitefriars complained that the smell of the river penetrated the odours of their incense, and that several of their brethren had already died from its 'putrid exhalations'. The inmates of the Fleet Prison were also killed by the waters encircling them. In 1560 a city doctor wrote that in the 'stinking lanes' in the vicinity of the Fleet, at the time of epidemic fever or plague, 'there died most of London, and were soonest inflicted and longest continued'. An outbreak of cholera in Clerkenwell Prison, in 1832, was also attributed to the presence of the effluent waters. It was one of the most defiled areas of the city.

Schemes have been proposed to allow the Fleet to flow again through the streets of London. A plan has been made to build an observation platform beneath Ludgate Circus, where the buried waters might be seen. The river has not entirely lost its hold upon the imagination of the city. On the corner of Warner Street and Ray Street, in the road before the Coach and Horses pub, a piece of grating can be found. If you put your ear close to it, you can still hear the sound of the river pulsing underneath. It is not dead.

6

The Heart of Darkness

In *Voyage au bout de la nuit* (1932) the French novelist, Louis-Ferdinand Céline, invokes *le communisme joyeux du caca*. This is to be translated as 'the joyous communism of shit'. There is no better preamble to the world of London's sewers. It is truly a journey into the night. The sewers are places of universal defilement, filled with matter that we have ejected from our bodies and flushed out of sight. They collect the waste of the world, left in streets or thrown down drains. They are the repository of primitive and repulsive, or simply outmoded, things. They represent putrefaction and dissolution.

Sewers were certainly the token of death. In a nineteenth-century report, it was concluded that if 'you were to take a map and mark out the districts which are the constant seats of fever in London . . . you would be able to mark out invariably and with absolute certainty where the sewers are'. The track of fever followed the contours of the underground. The several outbreaks of cholera in the city were closely identified with the course of these pestilential tunnels.

In London mythology the sewers contain fearsome underground creatures, among them rats as big as large cats. 'I've often seed as many as a hundred rats at once,' a nineteenth-century sewer-man confided. 'They think nothing of taking a man, if they found that they couldn't get away no how.' The tunnels sweat as if in a fever. Yet they may also be the womb of strange birth. In previous centuries excrement was used as a great fertiliser; schemes were proposed to take the contents of the London sewers and spread them over the adjacent countryside.

'The Rat-catchers', from Mayhew's *London Labour*, 1851

If there were sewers in Roman London, they have not survived. In the general model of Roman building they would indeed have existed. The original sewers of Rome itself lasted until 1913. There are Roman sewers in York. Yet in London they seem to have crumbled into decay and dust, leaving not one relic behind. It is not impossible, however, that they still lie buried beneath the modern city.

The sewers of early medieval London were the streams and rivers and ditches that ran down to the Thames. Cess-pits, lined with brick or stone, were also in common use and were cleansed weekly or fortnightly by urban workers known as 'gong-fermers'. In 1326 one of them, 'Richard the Raker', fell into his own cess-pit and suffocated 'monstrously in his own excrement'. The first pipes to carry waste, in an underground drainage system, were introduced to London in the thirteenth century during the reign of Henry III.

But they were not sufficient to contain the city's effusions. Mr William Sprot complained in 1328 that his neighbours, William and Adam Mere, had allowed their 'cloaca' or sewer to discharge its contents over his wall. Two Londoners were in 1347 accused of allowing their 'odours' to escape into an adjacent cellar. In 1388 an Act was passed to punish those 'who corrupt or pollute ditches, rivers, waters and the air of London'. It would have been easier to stop the tides of the Thames. As the city grew, so did its stench.

An Act of 1531 created a group of London officials known as 'commissioners of sewers', whose job it was to superintend the existing sewers and to create new ones. There were nine such commissions: for the City and Westminster, Holborn and Finsbury, Tower Hamlets and Greenwich, St Katherine's and Poplar and Blackwall. A large system of underground drainage was already in use, although it was intended to remove only surface water; house refuse was still collected in cess-pools and then distributed as manure or illegally dumped in the Thames.

A novel use for excrement was found in the late sixteenth century, when its nitrogen content was discovered to be useful in the manufacture of gunpowder. There arose a gang of workmen, known as 'saltpetremen', who were empowered to enter any house and remove all its excreta. It was complained by one member of Parliament in 1601 that 'they dig . . . in bedchambers, in sick rooms, not even sparing women in childbirth, yea even in God's house, the church'. It might seem, therefore, that London was sitting on a lake of shit. This may be one of the reasons why the concept of the underworld or underground still has offensive connotations.

In 1634, on the instigation of Inigo Jones, a large vaulted sewer was built in place of the open Moor Ditch.

After the Great Fire, when there was an opportunity to build anew, John Evelyn imagined an 'underground city' with 'all the vaults, cellars and arched Meanders yet remaining' to be connected with 'new erection'. The plan came to nothing. A series of local responses, however, tried to address the problems of pollution. The first brick sewers were built in the seventeenth century. The lower sections of the Fleet were arched over, and used as sewers, in 1727. A London Bridge sewer was constructed, using the Walbrook as its medium. Between 1756 and 1856 more than a hundred sewers were constructed beneath the streets. By that later date there were in London approximately 200,000 cess-pits and 360 sewers.

The new wave of construction yielded strange evidence of London's history. When workmen were digging up part of Smithfield, in the spring of 1849, in order to lay a new sewer, they came upon a mass of crude stone that was blackened by fire; the stones were covered with ashes and human bones. They had discovered the place of martyrdom in sixteenth-century London, where the Henrician and Marian heretics were burned to death. Many of the bones were removed as relics. The exact nature of the faith they once espoused, Catholic or Protestant, was not considered to be important.

The cess-pits and the new sewers were not entirely beneficial. Methane or swamp gas, generated by the cess-pits, often caught fire and exploded; those trapped in their houses were burned or suffocated. Many of the sewers were in a state of dilapidation. The bricks of the Mayfair sewer were said to be as rotten as gingerbread; you could have scooped them out with a spoon. Sewer-workers were suffocated by a gas, sulphurated hydrogen, that was the product of putrid decomposition.

A survey of the sewers of London was undertaken in the summer and autumn of 1848 when their condition was described as 'frightful'; the system was dilapidated and decayed, even dangerous. The sewer for the West-minster workhouse was 'in so wretched a condition that the leveller could scarcely work for the thick scum that covered the glasses of the spirit-level a few minutes after being wiped. ... A chamber is reached about thirty feet in length from the roof of which hangings of putrid matter like stalactites descend three feet in length.' One of the investigating party was 'dragged out on his back (through two feet of black foetid deposits) in a state of insensibility'. This was the heart of darkness, the lowest depth of a city that was already being described as a wilderness. It represented what was called a 'monstrous evil'.

Thus, in October 1849, four men were killed when entering an unventilated sewer in Kenilworth Road, Pimlico. In the same period an explosion at the

Kennington Road sewer injured some workmen with 'the skin peeled off their faces and their hair singed'. In November 1852, two men were instantly killed from poisonous air when they entered a sewer in Compton Street, Clerkenwell. In 1860 four men were suddenly killed in the Fleet Lane sewer by some unknown discharge.

Innumerable reports can be found of explosions caused by 'coal gas'. On 16 October 1833, a house in King Street, St James's Square, was the site of such an event. 'The gas appears to have made its way from the sewer up the drain into the house, and a servant entering with a light, it ignited; the room was filled with flame, the woman was lifted to the ceiling by the force of the explosion, which also blew off the skylight over the staircase.' The underworld was a place of threat as well as degradation. Its forces could find a way secretly into the outer world.

Yet underground London had already attracted its own clientele. A subterranean race of 'toshers' was born, people who earned their living by scavenging in the sewers for any items of value. They looked for pennies or sovereigns, or the fabulous ball of moulded coins known as a 'tosheroon'. They worked in silence and in stealth, closing off their bull's-eye lanterns whenever they passed a street-grating 'for otherwise a crowd might collect overhead'. Their work was of course illegal. They may also have been mistaken for an underground race coming up for air.

'The Sewer-hunter', 1851

They soon acquired a legendary quality, and became the object of sensational reports and descriptions. They were the beings of the underworld who entered the sewers on the banks of the Thames at low tide, armed with large sticks to defend themselves from rats. They carried lanterns to light their way, and wandered for miles beneath the crowded streets. They wore a distinctive uniform, with canvas trousers and long coats with large

72

pockets. They found metal spoons, iron tobacco-boxes, nails and pins, bones, marbles, buttons, pieces of silk, scrubbing brushes, empty purses, corks, candle-ends, seed, pieces of soap, false money and false teeth; these objects were the relics of Victorian London, scavenged by outcasts.

And how did these outcasts cope upon their quest? John Archer, in *Vestiges of Old London* (1851), reported that 'many venturers have been struck down in such a dismal pilgrimage'. Their role as pilgrims reinforced the notion that the tunnels and streams underground were still somehow sacred. Archer speculated that 'many have fallen suddenly choked, sunk bodily in the treacherous slime, become a prey to swarms of voracious rats, or been overwhelmed by a sudden increase of the polluted stream'. It is an apocalyptic fate. Henry Mayhew, in *London Labour and the London Poor* (1851), suggested that they were enveloped in darkness, 'their lights extinguished by the noisome vapours – till, faint and overpowered, they dropped down and died upon the spot'. That was the fate of the devotees of the underground gods, a race of supplicants doomed by their own calling. They were the pale votaries of darkness and excrement.

The dirtiest jobs do not change. The sewers of London are much the same as those first built at Knossos in 1700 BC, and the activities of sewer-workers or 'flushers' have been the same for thousands of years. In the nineteenth century it was reported that they actively enjoyed their work. The air of the sewers was supposed to be a sovereign defence against disease. The men preferred it to the atmosphere above the ground. Mayhew himself was surprised to note the good health of these underground workers; they were 'strong, robust and healthy men, generally florid in their complexion'. Yet he also described them as 'with a few exceptions stupid, unconscious of their degradation, and with little anxiety to be relieved of it'. This is the dismissive and contemptuous discourse of those above the ground.

'Flushing the Sewers', 1851

The words of the flushers themselves have often been reported. 'They was like warrens,' one sewer-man of the mid-nineteenth century recalled, 'you never see such shores [sewers]. ... It's pretty stuff, too, the gas, if you can only lay on your back when it goes "whish" an' see it runnin' all a-fire along the crown o'the arches. ... One mornin' when the tide was all right, we goes down to work, an' picks up a leg.' And, he added, 'Not a wooden one neither.'

Despite their bravado and their evident enjoyment of their work, they could not successfully deal with the damaged sewers or their contents. The 'great stink' issued forth in 1858. This was the period when the water closets of a quarter of a million households were directly connected to the public sewers, with the result that the waste was discharged immediately into the Thames. It became a river of effluent and an open sewer. The foreshore was black. Victoria and Albert embarked upon a pleasure cruise, but within minutes the smell had driven them back to the shore. The water supply of many Londoners was piped directly from the Thames, and was now described as being 'of a brownish colour'. The windows of the Houses of Parliament were covered with sheets soaked in chlorine, but they could not prevent the stench from what Disraeli called 'a Stygian pool reeking with ineffable and unbearable horror'. It was the 'unbearable horror' of the city.

Disraeli himself left a committee room of Westminster in some discomfort. 'With a mass of papers in one hand and with his pocket handkerchief clutched in the other, and applied closely to his nose, with body half bent, [he] hastened in dismay from the pestilential odour.' The underground world had invaded the surface. All that was ejected and rejected had come back with a vengeance.

The parliamentary authorities were now acutely aware that the sanitary conditions of the nineteenth century had changed not at all, and had in fact deteriorated, from the conditions of the fifteenth century. They were obliged to take general and immediate action. The chief engineer of the Metropolitan Board of Works, Joseph Bazalgette, found a solution. He proposed to build an elaborate system of sewers, running in parallel with the river, that would intercept the pipes going down to the Thames and carry the effluent beyond the city into 'outfalls' at Barking in north-east London and at Crossness south of the Thames on the Erith marshes. He also managed the reconstruction of the smaller sewers already in existence. The five principal intercepting sewers were at different depths, the lowest being some 36 feet beneath the surface.

Some were fearful at the enterprise of meddling with the underworld. They believed, according to an essay in *All the Year Round*, that the new sewers might become 'volcanoes of filth; gorged veins of putridity; ready to explode at any moment in a whirlwind of foul gas, and poison all those whom they fail to smother'. This is a vision of Hades let loose upon the outer world. Yet Bazalgette's work continued. Ford Madox Brown's painting of heroic labourers, *Work*, completed in 1863, depicts men laying an underground sewer in Heath Street, Hampstead.

Building techniques: a view from Wick Lane in Bow, 1860s

One of the lower sewers runs from Ravenscourt Park and Hammersmith to Kensington; it then proceeds beneath the Brompton Road and Piccadilly, and makes its hidden way along the Strand and Aldwych before going under the City and Aldgate. Another sewer starts at Hammersmith and begins its long journey towards the river Lea. It passes under Fulham and Chelsea before being propelled by a pumping station towards Millbank and the Houses of Parliament. From there it travels unseen beneath the Victoria Embankment, Blackfriars and Tower Hill, where it is directed to Whitechapel and Stepney. It has traversed the depths of London. In the tunnels themselves there is much elaborate architectural detailing and decoration, such as the graduated edging of the arches, even though the effects will rarely if ever be seen; it is almost Egyptian in its secrecy.

The whole system finds its quietus at the Abbey Mills Pumping Station in Stratford; the original building, now used as a 'back-up', was conceived in a style variously described as Venetian Gothic or Slavic or Byzantine as a suitably solemn tribute to the matter of the underworld. It was called 'the cathedral of sewage', again connecting the sacred and the underground worlds. Its sister station at Crossness was also described as a 'perfect shrine of machinery', with its interior resembling a Byzantine church. Abbey Mills was seen as a magical space, 'poetical' and 'fairy-like' according to a journalist from the *Daily Telegraph*, in the spring of 1865, thus confirming the underworld as a place of gleaming treasure. Yet the same journalist, entering the empty subterranean reservoir, also believed himself to be 'in the very jaws of peril, in the gorge of the valley of the shadow of death'; he was close to 'the filthiest mess in Europe, pent up and bridled in, panting and ready to leap out like a black panther'. The two images of the underworld, the magical and the demonic, are here conflated.

Bazalgette's Thames Embankment, 1867

In the spring of 1861, the *Observer* described Bazalgette's enterprise as 'the most extensive and wonderful work of modern times'. It was compared to the seven wonders of the ancient world. It encompassed 82 miles of main sewers, and over 1,000 miles of smaller sewers. It utilised 318 million bricks and 880,000 cubic yards of concrete. This is the system that, with improvements and extensions, is still in use. The brick, known as Staffordshire Blue, is intact within its bed of Portland cement. Bazalgette also realised that the flow of the river would be much increased if it were more narrowly embanked; so the Albert and Victoria Embankments were created. With Nash and Wren, Bazalgette enters the pantheon of London heroes.

It has been said that sewers exercise a curious fascination upon otherwise healthy and happy people. Many have undertaken the journey into Bazalgette's sewers in the role of tourists seeking sensations. They must be prepared for the descent, however, with the ritual of changing clothes; they wear waders that come up to the waist, woollen socks that reach the thigh, and white protective paper coveralls. A hard hat and a miner's lamp are also part of the equipment. They listen in silence to a recitation of rules and regulations. Their progress is equivalent to the journeys of classical mythology, where a living person travelled downwards into the realm of the dead before returning to the upper world with the tale of his or her descent. They are entering what is in a literal sense the wasteland.

A recent traveller went beneath Piccadilly in 1960

where 'down below it was like crossing the Styx. The fog had followed us down from the streets and swirled above the discoloured and strongly smelling river like the stream of Hades.' Another traveller described the Fleet sewer when seen fitfully by the light of the lanterns as 'one of the prisons designed by Piranesi'. That is one of the fears of walking under the ground; you may be trapped and imprisoned by the weight of the darkness. Sewers might induce fear and even hysteria.

The reports of the world beneath are written in a generally breathless tone, compounded of fear and awe. The underground chambers are compared to cathedrals, complete with pillars and buttresses, arches and crypts. One visitor, discovering an archway through which a cataract tumbled, remarked that it was as fantastic a scene as 'a dream of a subterranean monastery'. The travellers walk along tunnels that may reach a height of 17 feet, the cool tainted water lapping at about knee-height around their waders. Many are disconcerted by the pull of the water, and feel disoriented; they lose their equilibrium. They feel the sediment beneath their feet, as if they were walking on a beach at low tide. Great iron doors loom up at intervals, acting as valves. The noise of roaring water, somewhere in the distance, can generally be heard. It is the sound of cataracts and waterfalls. Yet the sounds of the outer world – the general roar and tumult of London – can also clearly be heard from the ventilator gratings in the roads above.

The travellers journey through great brick vaults where the various sewers join together. If they are unfortunate they might pass great deposits of fat fastened to the sides of the tunnels, some of them 30 or 40 inches thick; they have accrued from the ingestion of deposits of 'fast food'. Rats can occasionally be seen. They were more plentiful in the nineteenth and twentieth centuries, in what were known as blood sewers; these were the sewers under slaughter-houses and meat-markets.

The smell is sometimes offensive but often simply musty, with the odours of damp and stone; the atmosphere is close and clammy. A mist may hover over the turbid liquid. The vistas of brick in these curiously egg-shaped tunnels stretch ever onward. It would be easy to get lost. It would be easy to remain concealed. Some of the sewers have not been visited in the last fifteen years.

One nineteenth-century traveller reported that he saw, in an old sewer under Blackfriars Bridge, 'a cluster of mushrooms on the roof that were almost as large as ordinary soup-tureens'. On 28 July 1840, the first visitor to the newly bricked Fleet sewer descended at Fleet Bridge. 'I suspended my argand lamp on the breakwater of the sewer, and with my lanthorn light we proceeded towards the Thames.' It might be a narrative from the swamps of Borneo rather than the City of London. The sewer turned and twisted when suddenly, at a quarter to midday, they realised that the tide had come in to a depth of 2½ feet. He and his companions were in fear for their lives and 'holding our Lamps aloft, dashed up the Sewer, which we had to get up one half before out of danger. The air was close, and made us faint. However we got safe to Holborn Bridge. ... '

In *A Traveller's Life* Eric Newby reflected on a journey within the Tyburn sewer in the early 1960s. He was told to be alert to the presence of acetylene, petrol, carbon dioxide and hydrogen cyanide with 'a nice smell of almonds, the faintest suspicion of which sent any gang of sewermen' straight back to the surface at a very fast pace. Yet what caught his nostrils was the odour of coal gas, from leaking pipes, mixed with the unmistakable smell of untreated sewage. He noticed in the course of his journey families of rats nestling in broken brickwork. They were known to the sewer-men of the time as 'bunnies'. Newby was then taken into the Fleet sewer, where he was confronted by a warm and steamy darkness 'rather like a Turkish bath with something wrong with it'.

A visionary work of modern times, in the spirit of Bazalgette, is now being undertaken. The Thames Tideway Tunnel will run from Chiswick in West London to Beckton in East London, a distance of some 20 miles.

It will carry away the sewage and excess waste that accumulates after heavy rain, catching it before it reaches the river. It is being built 200 feet beneath the surface, following the sinuous course of the river, and must rank as one of the largest engineering projects of recent times. It is hoped to be completed by 2020. Yet, as in all matters of the underworld, it is not widely known or discussed.

Two other tunnels of water pass beneath London. A canal runs for three-quarters of a mile underneath the streets of Islington, snaking below Muriel Street, Barnsbury Road, Tolpuddle Street and Upper Street before coming out beside Noel Road. The second tunnel under London, the Maida Hill tunnel, runs under Edgware Road and proceeds beneath Aberdeen Place for 370 yards. The work on the tunnel was done by candlelight, and was constantly bedevilled by the discovery of underground springs; the excavated earth was taken to 'Mr Lord's field', that later became Lord's Cricket Ground.

The Islington tunnel was opened in 1820, and the first boats were propelled by 'legging', whereby men lay on planks and guided their craft with their feet and legs against the sides of the tunnel; they were replaced in 1826 by a steam tug that hauled the vessels through by means of a strong chain. There was a saying of the time, 'nearly gassed but nearly through'. A journalist recorded that this transport:

has a truly *tartarean* aspect. The smoke, the fire, and the noise of the engine contrasting with the black gloom of the arch, the blackness of the water, the crashing of the vessels against the sides of the tunnel and each other, and the lurid light that glimmers beyond each distant extremity form an aggregate of infernalia that must be witnessed to be adequately conceived.

Ready to start 'legging' in the Islington canal, 1930

The tunnel was renovated in 2000, and is now of course the avenue of boats with engine power. The experience of the journey, however, is the same. The voyage takes approximately twenty minutes during which the voyager, on a barge or a small boat, has the uncanny sensation of sailing beneath the city. It is possible to see a small circular light at the other end of the tunnel but then the darkness descends, described by one traveller as 'thick' and 'sooty'. The tunnel has its own weather. A pilot in the days of the steam tug remarked that 'when it's foggy outside it's clear in the tunnel.' It's a very queer tunnel.' The wind, in winter, blows very hard.

Opening a sewer by night, 1841

The Heart of Darkness

The sewers of London are now dangerous rather than deadly. The sewer-men work in teams under the command of a 'ganger'. They have their own patois, a kind of underground language, by which they identify themselves and their colleagues in the often treacherous conditions. They are at risk from Weil's disease, spread by rats, and from dizziness caused by working in the dark. They must also court the risk of explosion from the aggregation of gas or of drowning in a sudden storm of water. An hour's thunderstorm may precipitate an inch of rain, which is equivalent to 100 tons of water per acre. The first sign of calamity is a fierce wind that blows through the tunnels. This is followed by the deluge rushing down into the storm-relief sewers, with a force strong enough to carry away anything in its path. Sewers can never wholly be trusted.

7

The Pipes of London

Other pipes and tunnels run silently and invisibly beneath the surface of London. There was once a time when pipes of wood or leather carried water into London from the northern springs. By the thirteenth century, when some of the larger streams had run dry or had degenerated into open sewers, water was sent through pipes of lead; the slow dissolution of the metal must have had a noticeable effect upon the health of Londoners. In 1236 Gilbert de Sandford was granted 'liberty to convey water from the town of Tyburn by pipes of lead into the City'. This Great Conduit, as it was known, ran down what is now Oxford Street. Conduit Street marks its passage. It then turned into Holborn before eventually reaching Cheapside where it was discharged from a great pump known as 'the Conduit in Chepe'. A smaller conduit, built at the other end of Cheapside by Paul's Gate, was called 'the pissing conduit' by reason of its constant discharge of water. The system was, for the period, a remarkable feat of civil engineering, and the presence of the two conduits formed the emblematic centre of London at times of pageant or royal entry. They created a blessed space.

The Cornhill conduit, 1800

Other conduits were erected as the city expanded. White Conduit Street in Islington marks another source, while Lamb's Conduit Street in Holborn commemorates the benefaction of Sir William Lambe. A conduit known as the Standard rose on Cornhill, and was a landmark of the city. These conduits also became the home of ritual, like most sites of underground water. The mayor and aldermen would visit each one in turn; 'they hunted the hare and killed her' according to John Stow, before

89

enjoying a feast 'at the head of the conduit'. The banquet was followed by the hunting of the fox. These great pumps, however, proved to be a hindrance to the ever increasing traffic of the city; by the middle of the sixteenth century many of them had been removed.

Other sources of water were also deployed, most notably in the New River built by Hugh Middleton at the beginning of the seventeenth century. This flowed from Amwell and Chadwell Springs in Hertfordshire into North London. A fountain playing at the corner of Rosebery Avenue and Arlington Way, where once Thames Water had its headquarters and where Sadler's Wells still stands, marks its final destination. The shape of a great reservoir can still clearly be seen close by in Claremont Square. This is a very watery part of London. But the new river, like its older companions, has gone beneath the earth. It has been driven underground.

By the eighteenth century several water companies were laying pipes beneath the surface, with attendant problems of fierce competition and territorial struggle. Some London streets contained the pipes of three or four different companies vying for mastery. The companies joined together in 1811, but the subsequent monopoly did nothing to improve public health. Water flowed for very limited periods, sometimes as little as ten minutes each day, and there was no water on Sundays. Improvements were slow, gradual and random. Only at the beginning of the twentieth century, with the creation of the Metropolitan Water Board, was the public supply of water guaranteed. A huge water main was built, 19 feet beneath the surface, in 1955. This was followed, at the end of the twentieth century, by the construction of a ring water main lying at a depth of 130 feet; it encompasses the city in a loop of 50 miles, its central tunnel being some 7½ feet wide. It provides half of London's water, all of it moved by gravity alone. One of the great pumping stations that control the flow of water can be seen at Shepherd's Bush roundabout, where a towering pump has been installed. Beneath the traffic island, at the bottom of Park Lane, another pumping station has been built. You would never know that it was there.

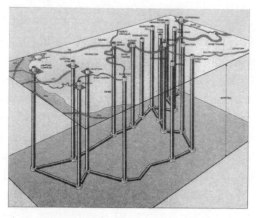

The London Water Ring Main

Another visionary scheme, from an earlier era, consisted in the provision of gas by means of pipes under the ground. The first of them was laid in the summer of 1805, when a newspaper described how 'the inflammable gas, which is quite transparent or invisible, began to flow into the pipes soon after eight o'clock'; a lamplighter lit each lantern in turn, instigating 'a clear, bright and colourless light' that would soon transform the streets of London. Shadow and darkness were banished from the main thoroughfares. 'It would have been a sight worth seeing,' Charles Dickens wrote in his weekly magazine, *All the Year Round*, 'the laying of the first gas pipe – and a picture worth drawing.' He believed that act to have been of more historical importance than the landing of Julius Caesar or the sealing of the Magna Carta. He had an essentially Victorian belief in power, and understood that gas would inaugurate a new order of things.

Yet there were serious misgivings about the nature of this new underground force. It was claimed that mounds of earth, each one the size of Primrose Hill, would be needed to keep the gas down. Fears of explosions were often expressed. Some of the pipes, from a myriad of new companies, were laid at too shallow a depth. In 1867 the Fenians – the Irish nationalists of the period – blew up a gas main in Clerkenwell as part of their campaign of terror in the 1860s, and a barrel of gunpowder was found beside a large gas-holder in Shoreditch. The largest

Beneath the streets, 1900

explosion of gas in the city occurred at the end of October 1865, when eleven workmen were killed by the accidental lighting of 1,000,000 cubic feet of gas at the London Gaslight Company. People walking a mile from the scene were thrown violently to the ground. The thing that lurked beneath, the thing that created terror, was now gas.

Water was once pumped, at a pressure of 400 pounds per square inch, beneath the streets of central London; it created hydraulic power, by means of which lifts rose and fell, safety curtains were drawn up and down, presses fired into action. By the early 1920s, 200 miles of hydraulic pipes had been laid beneath the surface of the city; the water has gone, but the pipes survive to carry other services such as cable and optic fibre networks. Ceramic pipes of the early nineteenth century were in time exchanged for cast iron. The nineteenth century was the age of cast iron, and its sturdy skeleton of services still lies beneath our feet. Cast iron was in part replaced by spun iron, and spun iron by serviceable polyethylene. But there are still many iron pipes in use for the transportation of gas; the last ones will not be removed until the spring of 2032.

A door within the plinth of the statue of Boadicea, on Westminster Bridge, leads to a tunnel some 6 feet in height that goes beneath the Embankment to all points east. This is the highway for a host of pipes, from the cables of the telephone companies to the pipes of the gas and water industries. Many such underground avenues weave beneath the streets. Nerve tunnels run from Piccadilly Circus to High Holborn, from Tottenham Court Road to the National Gallery, and from Islington to Soho. They all employ gratings for ventilation, through which can be seen the panoply of surface life; yet from this vantage the outer world somehow becomes alien and unusual. The oldest of these tunnels, beneath Garrick Street, was laid in 1861. They are all controlled by another 'circus' of installations beneath Piccadilly Circus. The life and activity beneath the streets are of immense size and complexity. Under the ground flow telecommunications, gas, drinking water, fibre optics, light, electricity, district heat mains, non-potable water, private wire networks and vacuum waste.

There are signals and pulses in the darkness beneath. London was the first city in the world to harbour an entire telephone system under the ground. The wires and cables went deeper and deeper, some of them carried through tunnels built by British Telecom and the London Electricity Board. Hundreds of thousands of miles of cable take electricity into every dwelling and place of work; it is the life force beneath the surface. The tentacles of the National Grid touch the cables at a number of points through the agency of 12,000 sub-stations that lower the voltage. The heat is so intense that every cable has to be well insulated.

Otherwise there would be a reprise of the situation experienced by John Evelyn in the autumn of 1666, after the

Great Fire, when 'the ground under my feet was so hot as made me not only sweat, but even burnt the soles of my shoes and put me all over in a sweat'. He contemplated an underground world where 'the very waters remained boiling; the voragos [abysses] of subterranean cellars, wells and dungeons formerly warehouses still burning in stench and dark clouds of smoke like Hell'. This is the heat now being exploited by a process known as 'underground thermal energy storage', by means of which excessive heat or cold can be stored in the earth for later use in public buildings. So the ancient earth can still become an agent of social change.

Yet the fear of fire and heat beneath the ground, the

Night workers laying an electric cable, 1930

definition of hell itself, still survives. The electric cables are buried in trenches, ducts, conduits and tunnels. They run through the tunnels of the London Underground, but small tunnels were also built for the purpose of holding them. Tunnels, for example, lie beneath the Thames. Other tunnels, some 80 or 90 feet beneath the surface, have recently been built; one of them runs under City Road, and another goes under the city itself. Forty feet beneath Leicester Square lies a vast electricity station on three levels. No one is aware of its presence, except for those who service it. It is entered by a small steel trap-door at the corner of Leicester Square and Panton Street, just to the left of the half-price ticket booth. It is disguised to baffle or to prevent unwanted visitors. The ticket office itself is the ventilation shaft for the operation. A new tunnel has been built by the National Grid beneath London, running from Elstree to St John's Wood; it is 12½ miles in length and almost 10 feet in width. It is known as the London Connection.

Our voices are carried beneath the ground. If they could be heard, a vast roar would echo and re-echo through the streets of London. British Telecom owns a region of the underworld, a domain crossed by thousands of miles of wires and cables running 100 feet beneath the earth. Many miles of tunnels pass in all directions beneath the capital, linking exchange with exchange. Fibre optic cables turn words and whispers into waves of light that flow beneath our feet.

8

The Mole Men

There are some people who seem to be born to dig tunnels. William John Cavendish-Bentinck-Scott, the fifth Duke of Portland in the middle of the nineteenth century, is best known for his obsessive desire to build a system of underground tunnels beneath his estate of Welbeck Abbey so that he could travel unobserved. He never wanted to be seen; he did not wish to speak to anyone, or even be noticed by his own staff. The underground world represented for him safety and invisibility. The moment of birth must have been deeply troubling for him.

In more recent times William Lyttle has built a system of tunnels, some of them 60 feet in length, beneath his property in Hackney. He had been at work upon this underground project for forty years, completely unknown and unobserved, until residents' complaints of inexplicable earth movements led to its discovery in 2003; the power of the adjacent street was one day terminated when he damaged a 450-volt cable. The tunnels and caverns radiate in all directions from his house in a subterranean web, but the meaning and purpose of the enterprise have never been discovered. 'Tunnelling,' he said to journalists, 'is something that should be talked about without panicking.' But that is precisely the response to someone who loves to inhabit the underworld – panic at the unknown. His nickname itself, 'the mole man', indicates the deep fear of transformation. This was the anxiety that created the Minotaur, half man and half bull, with his own kingdom beneath the earth.

It was reported in the press that Mr Lyttle's face 'lit up' when discussing underground chambers and secret tunnels, but it is hard to understand the origin of the fascination. It may be the comfort of being hidden, as in the case of the fifth Duke of Portland, and of somehow being safe from the depredations of the world. It may also represent a fantasy of power, whereby material or even spiritual strength is increased by being unknown and unseen. Before his retirement Mr Lyttle was an electrical engineer, harbouring the secrets of invisible power. To entertain the fantasy of the tunnel may represent the fear of being seen; and the power of being unseen.

When asked if he was an inventor Mr Lyttle replied that 'inventing things that don't work is a brilliant thing'. This is itself a brilliant answer, capturing the sheer facticity of much human activity. It is not purposeless. It has all the fascination of making art. The obsession, the act of digging out the earth, is enough. He went on to say that 'there is no secret', thus helping to demolish the fantasy that the underworld is somehow a secret place, a place of 'secret treasure'. He was simply creating more space, itself an instinctive human activity. He was creating a burrow.

One of the greatest of the mole men is Marc Isambard Brunel, whose dream of tunnelling beneath the Thames was eventually achieved at the expense of much cost and suffering. There had been two previous attempts to slay or undermine the deity of the river. In 1798 an engineer proposed to excavate a tunnel between Gravesend and Tilbury with 'a grand uninterrupted line of communication'; but the workers soon discovered quicksand, and the enterprise was abandoned. Four years later two Cornish engineers, accustomed to finding treasure under the ground, began to carve a tunnel out of the Thames clay between Rotherhithe and Limehouse; but their miners also found quicksand. They persevered, and the tunnel came within 120 feet of the shore before the river burst through.

The secret of Brunel's success lay in the humble mollusc, the *Teredo naturalis* or ship-worm. It is not clear whether he observed it in a prison cell, where he had been briefly consigned for debt, or in the naval yards at Chatham. Yet he did understand its life force. It eats the timber of a ship, instinctively creating more space like the mole man of Hackney, and then passes the wood through its body; its excreta are then used to bolster the fabric of the tunnel it has created. Brunel realised that the same process could be used on a much grander scale, with the invention of a massive *Teredo naturalis* made out of iron. As the engine advanced, the workers, in thirty-four separate 'cells' at the front, would carve out 4½ inches of clay at a time; a team of men in the rear would then line the newly uncovered piece of tunnel with brick and stone.

There was only one precedent. In 2180 BC the Babylonians built a tunnel beneath the Euphrates to unite the royal palace of Babylon with the temple to Jupiter Belos; after an interval of 4,000 years, the great work was about to begin again.

The chosen route beneath the river united Rotherhithe on the south bank with Wapping on the north. The work began on 2 March 1825 with the building of the first shaft to link the surface with the mouth of the tunnel. It was the shaft that claimed the first fatality when, four months later, a workman fell down through it and was killed. He was the first propitiatory sacrifice. The shaft descended gradually, through the force of its own weight, and nine months after its inception it reached the required depth of 75 feet beneath the surface of the river. This in itself was an extraordinary achievement of engineering. Work on the tunnel itself could now begin. The men were divided into two shifts, working for eight hours at a time and then resting for eight hours before beginning once more. They drank beer laced with gin, and they slept in what one miner called 'a feverish doze'.

Building the Tower subway, 1860s

The Mole Men

The river flooded the workings at the beginning of 1826, but the damp and darkness provoked symptoms that were variously described as 'ague' and 'dysentery'; one man succumbed to delirium, and died. This was the terror of the underworld. The miners truly believed that they might be buried alive. In the first days and weeks any unfamiliar sound echoing through the depths would send them running to the exit shaft. The temperature rose and fell alarmingly, sometimes swinging 30° at a time. One mistake, one faulty brick, might bring down the whole fabric. Explosions of gas occurred within the tunnel, also, so that the labourers lived in fear of fire as well as of water. The engineer in charge of the project collapsed from the strain of the undertaking. He was replaced by Marc Brunel's son, Isambard Kingdom Brunel.

The younger Brunel took over the work only to discover that the tunnel was coming close to the bed of the Thames. That part of the river was then packed with bags of clay, but they were not enough. In the spring of 1827 the Thames broke through once more; one workman died in the flood, and another died of fever and dysentery after the event. Marc Brunel was afflicted by the first of several strokes. The mythic horrors of the underworld had taken a large toll, and the elder Brunel himself considered that his men had been 'sacrificed' in their work of defying the natural world; they had entered a part of the underworld that had never before been visited. There were sometimes outbreaks of panic among the workers that had no discernible cause. On one occasion screams of 'Help!' were heard coming from the tunnel; a miner had fallen asleep and had dreamed of flooding.

At the beginning of 1828 the river once more inundated the workings; there were cries of 'The Thames is in! The Thames is in!' It was said that the ground above the tunnel seemed to come alive. Two men died in the deluge, but Isambard Kingdom Brunel was swept by the force of the water up the shaft to the surface. At the time of the calamity a parson from Rotherhithe deemed it to be 'a just judgment on the presumptuous aspirations of mortal men'. He might have repeated the words of God to Adam: 'Cursed is the ground because of you.' It was wrong to go beneath the earth, closer to the infernal regions. The project was discontinued, and was not revived until the advent of government money in 1835.

On their return to work, at the beginning of 1836, the miners were confronted by another horror of the underworld. They were digging their way through old earth that was heavily impregnated with foul gases, described by one of their number as 'vomiting flames of fire which burnt with a roaring noise'. Bright flame would burst from the face of the excavation.

Marc Brunel's diary is a litany of sorrowful mysteries. On 16 May 1838 he recorded the incidence of 'inflammable gas. Men complain very much.' Ten days later he wrote that 'Heywood [a miner] died this morning. ... Two more on the sick list. Page is evidently sinking very fast ...' The metaphor of 'sinking' is interesting; Page was going down even further than the others. Brunel also noted that 'the air is excessively offensive. It affects the eyes. I feel much debility after having been some time below. ... All complain of pain in the eyes.' Some of the workmen in fact suffered from blindness, temporary or permanent, that became known as the 'tunnel disease'. Epidemics of diarrhoea added their own horror to the polluted air. On 10 August 1838, the foreman of the works was escorted to a lunatic asylum where he could not be left unattended.

'It is truly distressing', Marc Brunel wrote to a friend, 'to see those men of ours who are disabled, not one leading man left of the first shift. Williams just gone off, complaining of fever, depression of spirits attended with acute pains in the head. The next to him, after two relapses, is, I have no doubt, completely gone, an excellent man. The evil is increasing ...' It was the evil of the subterranean depths. Eleven deaths occurred in the last two years of the enterprise. This was truly an unknown world, filled with peril. Nobody really understood what was happening.

There was no science of underground engineering. Brunel had merely copied the activity of a mollusc.

The Banquet in the Thames Tunnel, by George Jones, 1827. This was organised by Marc Brunel's son, Isambard Kingdom Brunel, to persuade people the tunnel was safe after the disastrous floods earlier in the year.

The Mole Men

When Fanny Kemble, the English actress, visited the work in progress she was much struck by the image of the miners, 'all begrimed, with their brawny arms and legs bare, some standing in black water up to their knees, others laboriously shovelling the black earth in their cages (while they sturdily sang at their task) with the red, murky light of links [flaming torches] and lanterns flashing and flickering about them'. They have become the creatures of the underworld, dwarves or devils, and Fanny Kemble instinctively draws the landscape of Hades.

Yet the drive for mastery of the lower world was maintained. The mid-nineteenth century has been described as the age of heroic materialism, and the Duke of Wellington described Brunel's enterprise as 'the greatest work of art ever contemplated'. The first subaqueous tunnel of the modern world was completed in the spring of 1840, and opened by Queen Victoria at the beginning of 1843. It was, for a time, the wonder of the earth. But the triumph was not what it seemed. The only entrance to, and exit from, the tunnel was by means of the vertical shafts on either bank. No room, or opportunity, existed for the vehicle traffic that had been envisaged. Many people visited the tunnel in the early months, eager for the sensation of walking beneath the Thames, but the popularity of the tunnel did not last.

It was disconcerting; it was even frightening. It was

pervaded by an air of hopelessness and dreariness, with the presence of the Thames above the brick arches as an imminent threat. 'The very walls were in a cold sweat', *The Times* reported upon the opening day, with the first visitors also afflicted by 'a lurking, chilling fear'. Nathaniel Hawthorne, who was then the American consul in Liverpool, recorded how he had descended through 'a wearisome succession of staircases' until he beheld 'the vista of an arched corridor that extends into everlasting night'. It was 'gloomier than a street of upper London' and seemed to him to have the fearful quality of a prison. Like any London prison it soon harboured its own particular inmates, with small stalls or shops set up in the alcoves of the tunnel by women who seldom or never saw any daylight.

But the Thames Tunnel also had other visitors. It was popularly supposed to be the haunt of thieves and prostitutes, taking over the unsavoury reputation of the Fleet Ditch; the underworld was once more calling to its proper denizens. It became known as 'the Hades Hotel'. It was an embarrassment, a shadow beneath the Thames, and in 1869 it was taken over by the East London Railway. In that capacity it has remained as an underground tunnel for the 'tube' ever since. The stairs of the original shaft were, until very recent times, in constant use by passengers.

The Entrance to the Thames Tunnel, by B. Dixie, 1836

The other tunnels under the Thames, confronting the primal fear of the river and of the darkness, have never lost their overwhelming sense of gloom. In 1869 a tunnel was built between Tower Hill in the north and Tooley Street in the south; it was made of cast iron rather than of brick, and was designed for the use of carriages drawn by cables from either end. Tower Bridge had not at this date been erected. The tunnel was as unsuccessful as its predecessor. If for some reason a carriage stopped in the middle of the tunnel, the passengers, in the sudden silence, could distinctly hear the sound of paddle steamers overhead. The river was too close. It was then turned into a pedestrian tunnel before being overtaken by the building of Tower Bridge. It has been employed ever since as a 'ghost tunnel', carrying the myriad cables and pipes that the city needs. If you enter it, you can hear the sound of the water churning overhead. It has the reputation of being one of the loneliest spots in all of London.

The same sensation can be experienced in the Greenwich Foot Tunnel, completed in 1902. It makes its way beneath the ground between Greenwich and the Isle of Dogs, and has remained a gloomy and intimidating place for more than a century. It is impossible not to feel the force of the water, some 53 feet above the pedestrian's head at high tide. The tunnel is lined with white tiles, and is always cool; it has an air of dankness. At a length of a quarter of a mile it is an unnerving space, with the constant fear of the tiles coming apart to make way for the deluge.

The tunnels beneath the river are filled with intimations of strangeness. The road tunnel known as the Limehouse Link, running beneath the ground from Tower Bridge to the Isle of Dogs, was opened in 1993. Its eastern and western portals bear two sculptures. One is entitled *Restless Dream* and the other is called *On Strange and Distant Lands*. A drive through the Blackwall Road Tunnel has variously been described as disquieting and intimidating. That is perhaps because of its proximity to the river; at some points it is only 5 feet beneath the water. The latest venture beneath the ground, the Docklands Light Railway's tunnel beneath the Thames between Island Garden and Cutty Sark, should also be experienced. Once the travellers are beneath the river they seem to be plunged into a deeper darkness, at once more intimate and more threatening.

More than twenty tunnels now burrow beneath the Thames, a larger number than in any other comparable city in the world; some of them are dry and disused, but their subterranean presence will endure as long as London itself.

9

The Deep Lines

The London Underground is an old system. Its pioneer and prime mover was born in the eighteenth century. The system itself was built before the unification of Italy and before the creation of Germany. Its first travellers wore top hats and frock-coats; there are early photographs of horse-drawn hansom cabs parked outside the underground stations. Oscar Wilde was a commuter on these subterranean trains, travelling from Sloane Square station to his office on *Woman's World* at the bottom of Ludgate Hill. Charles Dickens and Charles Darwin could both have used the Underground. The coffins of William Gladstone and Dr Barnardo were both transported beneath the earth in funereal underground trains. Jack the Ripper could have travelled on the Underground to Whitechapel; the station was served by the East London Railway. In the middle of the nineteenth century it was an astonishing thing. At the beginning of the twenty-first century, with the elaborate vistas of Canary Wharf or North Greenwich, it is still astonishing. It contains and commemorates many epochs.

The first begetter of the Underground, Charles Pearson,

advanced his proposals in the 1830s; by this period the main thoroughfares of London were blocked by an assortment of horse-drawn omnibuses, drays, phaetons and hackney carriages that carried hundreds of thousands of people into the city. As for the pedestrians, there was no counting them. Pearson considered that tunnels under London were the only solution to the congestion and delay above the ground, and suggested that underground routes should connect King's Cross with Farringdon Street. But so fanciful a conception invited only derision. A correspondent in *The Times* believed that a scheme for journeys beneath the surface was equivalent to absurd notions of flying machines and tunnels under the Channel. *Punch* and other magazines published cartoons in which the notion of an underground railway was ridiculed. 'We understand', *Punch* wrote in 1846, 'that a survey has already been made and that many of the inhabitants along the line have expressed their readiness to place their coal cellars at the disposal of the company.' It would turn into 'a Cheapside arcade for the penny hawkers' just as the Thames Tunnel had become.

More serious objections were raised. It would become a haven for Fenians and other terrorists, who would explode barrels of dynamite and destroy parts of the city. Several such explosions did indeed take place. The first of them was carried out by the 'Dynamiters' in 1881, when a charge of nitro-glycerine blew up in the tunnel of the District Line between Charing Cross and Westminster stations. There have been other such events ever since, most notably on the morning of 7 July 2005 when within fifty seconds three bombs exploded on three underground trains. The perpetrators were young Muslim men, but the motives for creating subterranean terror belong to no one faith. The fear of the underground is still very real. It is associated with the terror of an inferno beneath the surface, congruent to hell itself. Many escalator fires have started, most notably that in King's Cross in 1987 where twenty-seven people were killed. It was argued by some at the time that 'fires were a part of the nature of the oldest, most extensive, underground railway in the world'.

Pearson, a practical as well as an ingenious man, persisted in the face of objection and complaint. A parliamentary commission was established in 1846 to survey the state of the city's transport. Joseph Paxton submitted a scheme for an immense glass way circling above the streets and houses of London; the glass arcades, at a height of 108 feet, would provide lines for trains, and promenades for the people. It was a magnificent conception, but it was impractical. The only realistic scheme lay beneath the earth. It was granted to Pearson's Metropolitan Railway Company. Concerns were raised about ventilation within the tunnels but Isambard Kingdom Brunel, called as a witness, declared that the proposed journeys were very short. 'You need not take your dinner with you,' he said, 'or corn for your horse.'

At the end of January 1860 the first shafts descended at Euston Square and Paddington. 'In a day and a night,' one journalist wrote, 'a few hundred yards of roadway are enclosed, and a strange quiet reigns for a time, in consequence of the carriage traffic being diverted.' The omnibuses were diverted down alleys and back streets, where the outside passengers had to dodge street signs and barbers' poles. But then the navvies arrived with their steam engines and horses. 'The sound of pickaxes, spades and hammers, puffing of steam, and murmur of voices begin; never to cease day and night.' The method was that of 'cut and cover', by means of which an area was excavated before being once more covered by the road surface. London was in a ferment of fundamental change.

The path of the underground working was clear enough. It would run from Paddington to the Edgware Road before going under Marylebone Road and Euston Road; it would then use the valley of the Fleet in order to reach the City at Farringdon. The passenger to Farringdon still follows the same route as the travellers in Ben Jonson's 'Famous Voyage' of 1612. The ancient Fleet river, however, was not to be wholly ignored; in June 1862 it was reported that after heavy rain 'the black hole of the Fleet sewer, like a broken artery, poured out a thick rapid stream which found its way out fiercely . . . into the railway cutting'. The great brick walls of the tunnels rose upward with the force of the water.

The underground scheme itself was a force for destruction as well as improvement. The excavation of the valley of the Fleet destroyed a thousand homes and displaced 12,000 people who did not receive any compensation. They left their infested and infected tenements for a life of squalor elsewhere. That pattern of evicting the powerless and the poor continued throughout the construction of the underground railway in the nineteenth century. A magazine, *The Working Man*, made its own comment in 1860. 'Where are they gone, sir? Why, some's gone down Whitechapel way; some's gone in the Dials; some's gone to Kentish Town; and some's gone to the Work'us.'

By the autumn of 1861 the underground line was partially complete, and in the spring of 1862 a group of interested observers were drawn in wagons from Paddington to Euston Square. Gladstone and his wife were among the party. They were invited to inspect the newly completed tunnels, and were apparently much impressed by their novel and in many respects incredible journey 'under London'. It was worthy of a narrative by Jules Verne. It offered the perfect union of science, drama and romance.

On 9 January 1863, the Metropolitan Underground

Railway was formally unveiled. Pearson himself died a few weeks before the event. He had been born in the same month as Marie-Antoinette had perished on the guillotine, but he had inaugurated a service still in use in the twenty-first century. At the opening ceremony 700 dignitaries gathered at Paddington and were driven through the tunnels in a succession of trains; an engraving of *The Trial Trip on the Underground Railway* shows the open carriages filled with men waving their stove-pipe hats into the air as they are about to pass into a tunnel. When they eventually emerged into the terminus at Farringdon Street, they were greeted by police bands.

On the following day the line was opened to the public. The crowds, waiting for their first journey beneath the surface of the earth, were immense; the trains were filled immediately with the cry of 'No room! No room!' echoing through the underground halls. A few casualties were perhaps inevitable; the ventilation at Gower Street station was not sufficient, and two people were taken to hospital. A journalist wrote that 'it can be compared to nothing else than the crush at the doors of a theatre on the first night of a pantomime'. It was the first underground railway in the world, a wonder and a spectacle to rival anything upon the stage. Something of its appeal can still be seen on platform five of Baker Street, now restored to its pristine condition.

The Metropolitan Line was a considerable success, and carried approximately 30,000 passengers each day. So the trains were lengthened, and the intervals between them were reduced; they stopped for twenty seconds at each station before continuing their journey. They were driven by compact steam engines and accommodated three classes of carriage, the first class containing mirrors and carpets. They looked exactly like surface trains suddenly transported into the depths. Some complaints were of course made about the smoke and smell in the tunnels. The guards and porters sent a petition to the company, requesting that they be given permission to grow beards as a protection against sulphurous deposits. The locomotives themselves were given the names of tyrants – *Czar*, *Kaiser* and *Mogul* – or of voracious insects such as *Locust*, *Hornet* and *Mosquito*. This was a tribute to their power. One of them was named *Pluto*, the god of the underworld.

The first fatality occurred in the autumn of 1864. A railway guard at Portland Road station noticed a couple at the top of the stairs. He told them to hurry as the train was approaching. 'Come on, Kate,' the man said. The couple hurried down the steps. A short while later the body of the dying woman was found on the rails. She had been drinking with her companion, and had apparently fallen onto the line.

Gustave Doré's engraving of 'the worker's train', the Metropolitan Line,
from *London: A Pilgrimage*, 1872

The success of the Metropolitan encouraged other projectors and financiers to adopt similar schemes. London was consumed with underground fever. Fifty-three projects were put forward. The Great Western and Great Northern and Great Eastern railway companies were eager to move into the capital, while the Metropolitan itself was gradually extended in all directions from Swiss Cottage to South Kensington and Hammersmith. The District Line began constructing its own portion of what became the Inner Circle. 'The engineering world', the *City Press* reported in 1864, 'is literally frenzied with excitement about new railway schemes. We would as soon enter a lunatic asylum as attend a meeting of the Institute of Civic Engineers.'

Endless internal battles were fought between the underground companies, over such matters as routes and the width of tracks, but the enterprise of tunnelling beneath London went on. In 1865 Henry Mayhew travelled on an underground train in order to interview the passengers. A labourer told him that he used to walk 6 miles each day, to and from his place of work; now he was spared the inconvenience. He lived in Notting Hill, 'almost in open country', and thereby saved himself two shillings a week in rent.

The first tunnels to be literally bored beneath the earth, without using the 'cut and cover' method, ran from King William Street in the City to Stockwell in South London. The line opened in 1890, and since the journey was conducted entirely underground, the need for windows was deemed to be minimal. Only tiny slits were placed high on the sides. It was also feared that the passengers might panic at the sight of the walls of the tunnel rushing past them. The seats were quilted. So the carriages were known as 'padded cells'. A guard stood at the end of each carriage, and announced the names of the stations en route; he also called out warnings. 'Beware of card sharks on this train!' 'It is forbidden to ride on the roof!' The novel insertion of tunnels into the London clay led to the notion of 'the tubes' under the earth; soon enough they became known as the Tube, a name that has persisted ever since. When the Central Line was inaugurated in the summer of 1900 it became known as 'the Twopenny Tube' because of the flat price of the tickets.

Inside the 'padded cell' of the City and South London Railway

The building of these tunnels deep beneath the earth had dangers of its own; by the early years of the twentieth century they were bored by a rotary excavator that had knives at its front digging out the earth and depositing it onto a conveyor belt. Yet the atmospheric pressure at these depths was very high, and a report written in 1908 informed the Institution of Civil Engineers that 'a great deal of illness resulted among the men, but there were not many fatal cases'. The workmen were suffering from the disorder known to deep-sea divers as 'the bends'. On one occasion the air escaped through the bed of the

Thames and boiled 3 feet high above the surface, over-turning a boat.

The Fleet floods destroy the underground workings at Farringdon, 1862

The trains on the Stockwell Line of 1890 were the first to be powered by electricity, and thus it became the first underground electric railway in the world. It also provided another innovation. There were no first classes or second classes in this new world. All tickets were charged at the same rate, and all of the carriages were identical. It caused outrage in some quarters, and the *Railway Times* complained that lords and ladies would now be travelling with Billingsgate fishwives and Smith-field porters. Yet, as a reading of Dante would have suggested, all are equal in the underworld.

In the summer of 1867 a woman had dropped dead at Bishop's Road station on the Metropolitan Line, and an inquest resolved that she had died 'by natural causes, accelerated by the suffocating atmosphere of the Under-ground Railway'. By 1898, 550 trains were passing beneath the surface of London every day. A driver told a parliamentary commission that 'very seldom' was the smoke thick enough to obscure the tunnels. One chron-icler of the city recorded in his diary for 23 June 1887 that 'I had my first experience of Hades today'. He was travelling between Baker Street and Moorgate, but the windows of the carriage were closed to lessen the effect of the smoke and sulphur in the tunnels. He added, however, that 'the compartment in which I sat was filled with passengers who were smoking pipes, as is the English habit'; as a result he was 'near dead from asphyxiation and heat'. In 1897 one passenger was almost overcome with the fumes, and was escorted up to the street and a nearby chemist's. The chemist looked at him for a moment. 'Oh I see,' he said, 'Metropolitan Railway.' He poured out a glass of some remedial mixture. The passenger asked him if he had many such cases. 'Why bless you, sir,' he replied. 'We often have twenty cases a day.' A proposal was made to place evergreen shrubs on the station platforms, to reduce the effect of carbonic acid, but it was not accepted.

Some claims were made that the atmosphere of the Underground had benign effects, just as the sewer workers of the period believed that their labours rendered them healthier. The underworld may be seen as a source of strength. The fumes were so beneficial that Great Portland Street station was 'used as a sanatorium for men who had been afflicted with asthma and bronchial complaints'. Acid gas was said to cure tonsillitis. It was also reported that an anorexic suddenly developed a ravenous appetite after a single journey on the Twopenny Tube. It was something to do with the temperature of the tunnels.

The effect of the smoke, however, was to accelerate demands for electric traction that had proved so successful on the Stockwell Line. In 1905 the Inner Circle was converted for the use of electrical trains, and soon enough other lines were electrified. The days of the underground steam engine were over. Comfort could be purchased at a price. By 1910 a sixpenny ticket allowed the traveller access to the first-class carriages of the Metropolitan Railway's Pullman cars; the carriages contained morocco armchairs set in the replica of a drawing room with mahogany walls. Electric lamps were placed on side-tables, and blinds of green silk covered the windows. Breakfast, lunch and dinner were served.

In 1911 the first escalator was introduced at Earls Court station, to unite the platforms of the District and Piccadilly Lines. The promotional literature promised that the passenger 'can step on to the stairlift at once, and be gently carried to his train. A boon that the mere man will also appreciate is the fact that he will not be prohibited from smoking, as in the lift, for the stairlift is made entirely of fireproof material.'

A porter was employed to shout out, through a device known as a stentorphone, 'This way to the moving staircase! The only one of its kind in London! NOW running! The world's wonder!' Some travellers screamed at the prospect of alighting from the moving steps, and placards invited them to 'step off with the left foot'. A man with a wooden leg was employed to ride up and down the escalator to instil confidence in the nervous passengers. It was, according to a contemporary report, 'as good as a joy-wheel'. An experimental spiral escalator was installed at Holloway Road tube station by an American company, but it was never used. Yet this was an extraordinary new world beneath the surface of the capital.

So the lines grew and grew. The Inner Circle was complete, and in the first years of the twentieth century it took seventy minutes to journey around the circuit by steam train; a hundred years later, the trains are only twenty minutes faster. By 1907 the Baker Street and Waterloo Line had reached Edgware Road, and was known as the 'Bakerloo'; the name was considered to be vulgar and a 'gutter title'. The line between Holborn to the Strand was opened in the same year, and was eventually named the Piccadilly Line; the Charing Cross, Euston and Hampstead railways were merged into one large company called the Metropolitan District Electric Traction Company. This conglomerate had already begun to build its own power station at Lots Road, by the Thames at Chelsea, in order to provide power for the newly electrified service.

At work in the 'Shield', Great Northern and City Railway, 1920s

The Deep Lines

Like the city above, the Underground grew haphazardly and pragmatically; it was not planned logically or as a whole. Many levels were in place, many lines converging and diverging, with corridors and stairways, lifts and escalators comprising the pieces of an infernal or divine machine. Tunnels were built ever deeper. New stations were erected, and older stations abandoned. It was guided by the imperatives of money and of power, rather than the interests of the citizens. In the first instance it was administered by capitalist financiers of dubious reputation. That is the London story.

In 1908 a meeting of the various subterranean companies was convened to find a common name for their enterprise. The choice was between 'Tube' and 'Electric' and 'Underground'; the last was chosen. This was the time when the 'bull's-eye' device was first used as a symbol for the service.

The system was in place, and remained largely unaltered until the 1960s when the Victoria Line was constructed. It was the first new line across central London in fifty years and acted as a service network, with each of its stations connecting to another line or to a surface terminus. In the course of its construction fossils buried fifty million years before were discovered. They now reside in the Natural History Museum. Their discovery is another indication of the depth at which the tunnels were laid; the lowest depth of the Underground system lies 221 feet beneath Hampstead Heath, where the Northern Line runs. At Westminster station the Jubilee Line, the most recent to be built, lies 104 feet beneath sea level. At this point the clay surrounding the tunnels absorbs the heat and stores it, gradually becoming hotter and hotter; temperatures of 65° Fahrenheit (18.3° Celsius) have been recorded in the adjacent earth. So ventilators were required to keep the temperature at an average of 70° Fahrenheit (21° Celsius); but in the recent years of expansion the heat within the earth has risen once more, and the average temperature of the deep level tubes is now (86° Fahrenheit 30° degrees Celsius). Underground is 10° warmer than overground.

The Victoria Line was succeeded by the Jubilee Line, originally to be called the Fleet Line since its route followed the path of the ancient river. But in 1999 it was directed towards parts of South London that the underground had not previously reached; it now reaches its quietus, having passed through its southern stretch, at its eastern terminus in Stratford. In the course of its excavation it traversed the ground beneath the oldest parts of London. The line travelled back 5,000 years. In the depths of the new system were uncovered pieces of Neolithic pottery and Roman tiles, a twelfth-century quay, a thirteenth-century gatehouse and a fourteenth-century wool market. Mosaic floors, and painted walls, have also been identified. When the Jubilee was taken beneath Southwark High Street it found an older street, dating from AD 60, lined with houses of clay or timber; ruts were observed in the street, made by carts and chariot wheels. Now the commuter, or passenger, passes over them at a different speed. When the line went out to Stratford it unearthed an Iron Age settlement and a Cistercian monastery of the twelfth century. 'It's chaotic down there,' the architect of the Jubilee Line extension said, 'you can't believe what's going on.'

The Tube is still in large part an old place. It is Victorian. Abandoned tunnels run nowhere, known as 'dead tunnels', snaking their way through the living system; they are sometimes damp, and sometimes dusty, with the patina of past time along their walls and floors. The tunnels beneath the Thames have a layer of moss that has somehow grown across the sheets of metal panels. The danger of flooding is still great; many hundreds of pumps discharge 6,600 thousand gallons of water each day in order to preserve the system.

The Underground curves and swerves beneath the surface, some tunnels in a constant state of movement. The tunnels beneath the City of London still follow the medieval street plan in order to curb the risk to ancient buildings. They are also a vast reservoir of mortality, with large amounts of human hair and skin to be removed each night between 1.00 and 5.00 in the morning. These are the only hours when the Underground rests. Metal staircases, and chambers, and abandoned shafts, lie beneath the ground; there are brick arches, of the same construction as the nineteenth-century sewers. The Underground might therefore be seen as a sewer, through which people are sluiced. That is why, at the beginning of the enterprise, *The Times* doubted that Londoners would ever wish 'to be driven amid palpable darkness through the foul sub-soil of London'. The Waterloo and City Line, opened in 1898, was known as 'the Drain'.

Yet the Tube system, 150 years old, is ever renewed. It resembles London itself in its capacity for growth and change. Baker Street was opened in 1863, and is still crowded with travellers. In 2007 the whole system carried 1 billion passengers. It is bewildering, but it has been reduced to order in the now famous 'Tube map' that has become an emblem of the city itself.

If in 5,000 or 10,000 years' time the map of the Underground is uncovered, its purpose and meaning might be irrecoverable. There will be debate over the precise significance of 'white city' and 'seven sisters', 'gospel oak' and 'elephant and castle', but the principle of the red and blue and green lines may be lost upon our remote descendants. It is not really a map at all, and is described by the social historian Eric Hobsbawm as 'the most original work of avant-garde art in Britain between the wars'. An abstract created by an Underground employee, Henry Beck, in 1931, it reminds some of Mondrian, and others of a diagram for electrical wiring. Beck himself did work in the signalling department, where he devised circuits for the current. Yet his design is simple, clear and memorable; it gives an air of rationality to what is in reality a haphazard and chaotic system. The city itself is identified as a series of horizontals, verticals and diagonals with the greatest emphasis upon central London. 'If you're

People waiting for the lifts at the Bank underground station on the Central Line in 1901.

going underground,' he said, 'why bother with geography?' So he presents a utopian vision of the capital.

The architecture of the Underground has also had a significant history. The first stations resembled vast basilicas with arches and alcoves fitfully lit by gaslight. In its early days the ticket office of Bank station was located in the crypt of St Mary Woolnoth, thus contributing to the sense of sacred space. Baker Street station itself was described as having 'a gloomy, catacomb-like appearance'. Some people were awed, and some frightened, by the journey into these smoking caverns beneath the earth. The walls of the stations were plastered with advertisements for Nestlé's Milk, Bovril, and other commodities. Above ground these early stations were built of white brick with slate roofs and stone dressings. Other stations were given a Moorish, or a Gothic, tone. The City and South London Railway preferred to construct great domes to house the workings of the lift shaft, complete with cupola and weather vane. They are still to be seen, as at Clapham Common.

The Baker Street and Waterloo Railway, at the beginning of the twentieth century, erected single-storey stations faced and decorated with moulded terracotta blocks of red, known as 'ox-blood'; the shining tiles can still be seen in stations such as Gloucester Road and the now disused Strand. The association between the underworld and animal sacrifice has been maintained. A wall of these blood-red tiles can be found off the Brompton Road beside the Oratory; it marks the spot where the Brompton Road station once stood. These ox-blood bricks are in sharp contrast with the light brick-work of the District Line stations, erected in the same period. Within the station itself the motif changed to one of bottle-green tiles, with the upper walls of white plaster.

The cupola of Clapham Common station, 1930s

In the 1920s the Hampstead Line developed a style that became known as 'suburban classical', with the stations graced by coupled Doric columns carved out of Portland stone. The pitched roof, of pyramidal shape, was covered with red Italian tiles so that the stations resembled Roman villas of an earlier date. They provided what one pamphlet described as an 'inviting doorway' into the world beneath the ground. The City and South London Railway, in the same period, preferred stark cubic forms of Portland stone that resembled Aztec temples. They can still be seen at Hounslow West and at Tooting Broadway. Within the ticket hall of Hounslow West are laid elaborate tile friezes which conjure up an air of geometrical frenzy; the total effect resembles that of a sarcophagus. Such stations can still provoke a sense of unease.

When in 1930 the Piccadilly Line began to stretch northwards towards Cockfosters, twenty-two tunnelling shields were mustered for the underground work. In the process some of the most memorable underground stations were built under the influence of Walter Gropius and the Bauhaus movement; the bold cylindrical or rectangular shapes, as, for example, at Arnos Grove and Sudbury Town, became instantly recognisable as portals to the underworld. Interior lighting was subtly modified to introduce a warmer mood into the otherwise bleak surroundings. Opal glass shades, and reflectors, cast a more even glow.

They were believed to promote the concept of 'night architecture', being as visible in the darkness as in the light. They were the last of the truly innovative stations of the twentieth century, but they were perhaps no more welcoming than their predecessors.

The art of the Underground has an honourable place in the culture of London. The traveller descends slowly into an animated world of signs and posters. Some of the advertisements along the escalator are now moving films, bold and garish. The colourful and sometimes strident posters on the walls of the stations continue a tradition as old as the Underground itself. The passenger is surrounded by vibrant line and colour. The murals of David Gentleman at Charing Cross display the stages by which the masons and craftsmen of the late thirteenth century created the Eleanor Cross beyond the station. (In fact the cross is a replica, and is in the wrong place.) The head of Sherlock Holmes adorns the tiled walls of Baker Street station. The mosaics of Eduardo Paolozzi decorate the walls of Tottenham Court Road station.

The gateways to the underworld have also been embellished with striking images. A statue of an archer surmounts East Finchley station, conceived in a style strongly reminiscent of ancient South American civilisations. His bow is aimed directly down the length of the tunnel. Griffins were carved into the walls of Aldgate

David Gentleman's murals on the Northern Line platforms at Charing
Cross, 1979, showing the building of the Eleanor Cross

East, St Paul's, and other stations; the griffins were the
monsters that protected gold mines and buried treasure,
and thus suitable creatures to guard the Underground. A
figure of Mercury is to be found over an entrance to
Bank station, and a cherub once stood above Oxford
Circus.

The latest extensions of the Jubilee Line, south of the
river, have been rendered memorable by some of the most
striking architecture in contemporary London. Canary
Wharf and North Greenwich, designed by Norman Foster
and Will Alsop respectively, are triumphs of postmodern
engineering. They are the dramatic portals into the underworld, and at the time of completion were described as

secular cathedrals. With their vast canopies of glass and underground caverns of steel, they represent the force of the collective will and the great general drama of the human spirit. It is the spirit of the Underground itself.

10

Far Under Ground

Certain people are afraid of the Underground. The journey under the earth inspires panic and claustrophobia. It induces dreams of fire and suffocation. You may experience what has been called the fear and madness of crowds. Once you are immersed in this other-land, removed from the familiar world, you may suffer from inexplicable terrors.

It is a solitary experience, even though you are never alone. There is nothing joyful about the proximity to a hundred or a thousand individuals estranged one from another. The Underground is a deep pool of individual solitudes. Somehow 'I' is now indistinguishable from 'them'. It is a profoundly egalitarian, or flattening, process.

Among 'them' may be drunks, or beggars, or the mad; even the busker, strumming his or her guitar, may seem to be a threat. That is why most travellers are hurried in the Underground; they wish to arrive at their destination as soon as possible. The Tube system is devoted to finding the shortest route possible between two locations. It is not really a place at all. It is a process of movement and expectation.

Experienced travellers know the contours of each station, just as a traveller on the surface knows a short cut or a convenient crossroads. They take pleasure in their speed and agility; they know where to stand in order to gain immediate access to the train; they know which carriage stops nearest to an exit. The journey therefore becomes habitual, a part of the traveller's mental as well as physical history. It becomes a ritual. The wonder and excitement, experienced by nineteenth-century travellers, have gone.

The Underground is in many respects a symbol of collective will. It is both solitary and communal, representing the paradox embedded in any society or culture. It eases the passage of individual lives, but it is also a communal force with its own public codes and demands. It can therefore be seen as an oppressive system, part of the worktime nexus of contemporary capitalism. It is an ideological, as well as a sociological, construct. The commuter of the morning 'rush hour' is part of a system of constraint and obligation. 'We do not ride on the railroad,' Thoreau once said of the new railway system in America, 'it rides upon us.'

The Underground is also a place of collective memory. The names of the stations prompt historical associations. Tower. St Paul's. Bank. Victoria. Waterloo. G. K. Chesterton noted that St James's Park, Westminster,

Poster by Alfred France, 1911

Charing Cross, Temple and Blackfriars 'are really the foundation stones of London, and it is right that they should (as it were) be underground' since 'all bear witness to an ancient religion'. The passenger travels within the origin of the city. It is a curious fact that the further the train moves from the centre of the city, the more anonymous it becomes. The journey becomes less intense. It becomes less intimate. It loses its mystery.

Yet every line, and every station, has its own particular identity. The Northern Line is intense and moody, while the Central Line is filled with purpose and energy. The Circle Line is adventurous and breezy, while the Bakerloo Line is disconsolate and brooding. The sorrows of Lancaster Gate are preceded by the liveliness of Notting Hill Gate, while the comfort of Sloane Square is followed by the brisk anonymity of Victoria. Underground trains have a different tone, and atmosphere, at distinct times of day. In the afternoon, for example, when 'everyone else' is at work they become more seductive and luxuriant places redolent of ease or even indolence. In the late evening they become more sinister, a haven for the drunk or the mad.

The Underground can also be the haunt of furtive desires. It can be a place of chance encounters and of secret meetings, with all the pressure of the old earth lending more fervour to the scene. In the twentieth century Lancaster Gate was known as an assignation place for homosexuals. An incoming train might be described as a wheel of fortune for those in search of partners. To be alone is to become an adventurer, or a predator.

In *The Soul of London* (1905) Ford Madox Ford wrote that 'I have known a man, dying a long way from London, sigh queerly for a sight of the gush of smoke that, on a platform of the Underground, one may see, escaping in great woolly clots up a circular opening, by a grimy, rusted, iron shield, into the dim upper light.' He is like a prisoner dreaming once more of his confinement. Yet the smoke has a familiar and reassuring smell.

The Underground itself has a faintly sour, faintly singed, odour. It resembles the smell of hair cut with electric blades. There is also the taint of dust, largely comprised of human skin. If electricity had an odour it would be this. John Betjeman, in *Summoned By Bells* (1960), recalled that in the 1920s the Central Line had the odour of ozone; but it was not a natural smell emanating from the sea or from the seaweed. It was not of the ocean. It smelled of a chemical manufactured in Birmingham.

His memory was very accurate. The administrators of the Underground had decided to pump ozone onto the platforms to counteract the sour smell of the tunnels. It was a bizarre attempt to make the world beneath the surface smell of the sea from which it had once emerged. It made commuters slightly ill. Betjeman, on another occasion, recalled 'the pleasant smell of wet earth and graveyards that used to hang about the City and South London Tube railway'.

The sights, and sounds, of the Underground are unique and identifiable. A sudden wind announces the imminent arrival of a train, accompanied by the subdued roar of the approach. A clatter of footsteps echoes in the corridors of white tile, together with the subdued jolting rhythm of the escalator. Yet what if there is no sound? What then? A silent station is a disquieting and even a cursed place. The forty-four disused and forgotten stations of the system are known as 'dead stations'. The earth is the place for the dead, is it not?

A traveller, going west just past Holborn station, may catch a glimpse of tiled walls. They are the last vestiges of a station once known as British Museum. The tiles of Down Street station can also still be seen as you journey underground between Green Park and Hyde Park Corner; above the ground, in Down Street itself, the ox-blood tiles of terracotta mark the spot of the long-forgotten station. King William Street station, abandoned in 1900, still has posters on its walls. Mark Lane can still be seen between Monument and Tower Hill; North End, the deepest of all stations, can be glimpsed as if in reverie between Hampstead and Golders Green. The platforms of Brompton Road, however, have been closed off and shielded from the gaze of passing travellers.

A station once stood between Camden Town and Kentish Town, named South Kentish Town. It is said that an unwary traveller alighted here when his train was stopped by a signal. He found himself alone on a dark and abandoned platform, where he was marooned for a week. He was only rescued when he caught the attention of a passing driver by burning some advertising posters. It is an unlikely story, but it captures the fear of being trapped in a system from which there is no obvious escape.

Dead stations are also known as 'ghost stations', and of course one or two of them have been credited with wraiths and apparitions. Ghosts are quite at home in the underworld. The shadows of the dead have always been supposed to walk beneath the surface of the earth. The Underground system passes through many burial grounds and plague pits. Deaths have occurred in the course of its construction. Murders, and suicides, have occurred on the various lines.

So the ghosts are supposed to walk. A phantom of a man has been seen by various station officials on the platforms of Covent Garden; he is described as 'a slim oval-faced man wearing a light grey suit and white glasses'. The sound of running steps has often been heard at Elephant and Castle, with the additional claim that the steps always seem to be running *towards* those who hear them. Certain drivers have complained about the 'loop' between Kennington and Charing Cross; it is said that it has a disconcerting atmosphere. When Vauxhall station was being built on the Victoria Line, in 1968, a number of workers saw a man approximately 7 feet in height wearing brown overalls and a cloth cap. He was never identified. The passengers of the Bakerloo Line are particularly liable to see unannounced visitors. There have often been reports of the reflection of a face in the window, when no one is sitting in the opposite seats.

This has also been the theme of ghost stories set on the Underground. In one of them, R. Chetwynd-Hayes's *Non-Paying Passengers* (1974), the protagonist sees the reflection of the face of his dead wife. In *Bad Company* (1956) Walter de la Mare invokes the presence of a ghost in one of London's 'many subterranean railway stations'. On the platform 'the glare and glitter, the noise, the very air one breathes, affects nerves and spirits. One expects vaguely strange meetings in such surroundings. On this occasion, the expectation was justified.'

Unlucky stations can be found. Moorgate, the site of a train disaster in 1975 in which fifty-six people died, has always been the object of rumours about hauntings. In the autumn of 1940 many people were caught in a fire at the same station, after a bombing raid, when the heat was so intense that the glass and aluminium doors had dissolved. In the winter of 1974 a gang of engineers reported that they had seen a figure in blue overalls approaching them; as he came closer they saw that he had an expression of abject horror. He then disappeared. The driver of the fatal train in February 1975, approaching platform nine, was described as 'sitting bolt upright in his cabin, hands on the controls, staring straight ahead'. He simply drove into the wall of a dead-end tunnel.

Suicides prefer to die beneath the earth. It is estimated that there are three attempts each week, one being successful. More deaths occur in underground than in overground stations. The favourite time of day is 11.00 a.m., and the most popular venues are King's Cross and Victoria. Deep pits are built beneath the rails, known as 'catch pits' or 'suicide pits', to contain and save the people if they fall through. The suicides are known as 'jumpers' and, after each such attempt, an announcement comes over the loud-speakers calling for an 'Inspector Sands' to investigate an 'incident'. The roar of the train entering the station may be construed as an invitation to leap.

A general air of depression seeps through the walls of

the Underground. In a memoir of one erstwhile Underground worker, Christopher Ross's *Tunnel Visions* (2001), there is an account of the 'very low morale' among those who work beneath the earth; the atmosphere is 'negative'. The spirits of some workers may not noticeably be raised by the fact that they are not needed; the Central and Victoria Lines are fully automatic, so that the drivers sit in front of the trains as some kind of theatrical prop to instil confidence in the travelling public.

The literature of the nineteenth and twentieth centuries has often embodied what was once known as the 'romance' of the Underground. In Rose Macaulay's *Told by an Idiot* (1923), two young people indulge in the pleasure of going around and around the Circle Line as if it were a circus wheel. 'Two penny fares. Down the stairs into the delicious, romantic, cool valley. ... Oh joy! Sing for the circle completed, the new circle begun.' In Helen de Witt's *The Last Samurai* (2000) mother and young son also revolve around the Circle Line for the sake of its warmth; they take with them piles of books, including the *Odyssey* and the *House at Pooh Corner*.

For some writers the Underground was the locale for otherwise buried passion. The hero of H. G. Wells's *Tono-Bungay* (1909) takes a young lady on 'the underground railway' and in an otherwise empty carriage kisses her on

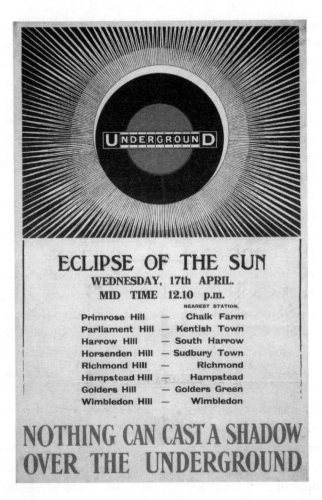

Poster by Charles Sharland, 1912

the lips. Such behaviour was only permissible under the earth. To fornicate is to behave as people do in the vaults, known as *fornices* in Latin. A more discreet version of this experience is recounted in Henry James's novel, *A London Life* (1889), when a young man and an American woman agree to walking in 'a romantic, Bohemian manner . . . and taking the mysterious underground railway' from Victoria. 'No, no,' the American lady says, 'this is very exceptional; if we were both English – and both what we are, otherwise – we wouldn't do this.' A journey of the sexes beneath the ground somehow constitutes an alien experience.

In *A Word Child* (1975) Iris Murdoch described the buffet on the west platform of Sloane Square, known as 'The Hole in the Wall', where alcohol was served. It was one of three or four such places. 'Drinking there between six and seven in the shifting crowd of rush-hour travellers,' she wrote, 'one could feel on one's shoulders as a curiously soothing yoke the weariness of toiling London.' She experienced the weight of the multitude in the bowels of the earth, soothing because it is shared by all equally. These bars were for her 'the source of a dark excitement, places of profound communication with London, with the sources of life'. They were the watering holes of Pluto's kingdom.

When in the spring of 1897 *The Idler* published a

weekly serial featuring a murderer on the loose in the trains under the earth, the number of Underground travellers dropped markedly. The adventures had hit upon a nerve of real fear. In Baroness Orczy's *The Mysterious Death on the Underground Railway* (1908) a woman is killed in a carriage of the Metropolitan Railway at Aldgate station. The murderer cannot be found, an emblem of the essential anonymity of the Underground that was confirmed in the unsolved real killing of Countess Teresa Lubienska who was stabbed to death at Gloucester Road station in 1957. In an underworld where everyone's identity is in large part concealed, how will a suspect ever be captured?

In *The Mysteries of Modern London* (1906) George Sims speculates on the identity of a passenger who 'travelled to Whitechapel by the underground railway, often late at night. Probably on several occasions he had but one fellow passenger in the compartment with him, and that may have been a woman. Imagine what the feelings of those travellers would have been had they known that they were alone in the dark tunnels of the Underground with Jack the Ripper?' There are no individuals in the Underground; there is only a crowd. In John Galsworthy's *Man of Property* (1906) Soames Forsyte enters the Tube at Sloane Square and notices that 'these shadowy figures, wrapped each in

The police find the body of Catherine Eddowes in a Whitechapel
cellar, murdered by Jack the Ripper in 1888

his own little shroud of fog, took no notice of each other'.

A project known as 'Alight Here', established in 2010, has been established to collect any poems inspired by London's Underground stations. It is indeed the proper material of poetry. Seamus Heaney's 'The Underground', for example, employs the myth of Orpheus and Eurydice in the context of vaulted tunnels and lamplit stations.

There are films, too, that speculate upon the shadows cast by the world underground. In *Death Line* (1972) (distributed as *Raw Meat* in the United States) a troglodytic race preys upon unwary travellers; this is an enduring fantasy of the Underground, and has taken many forms. It exploits the fear that many disturbed or dangerous people prefer to live beneath the earth. In *The Mysterious Planet* (a 1986 serial in the *Doctor Who* dramas) set in the remote future, a race of humans lives among the ruins of Marble Arch station. In *Quatermass and the Pit* (1967) an alien spacecraft is found buried deep in an Underground station named Hobbs End; this is a genuinely disturbing film in which all the associations of the underworld, with death and with the devil, are fully exploited.

Anthony Asquith's *Underground*, a silent film made in 1928, is an invaluable record of the Tube system at a relatively early date. The hero is a young official of the

Underground, and the villain is an employee at Lots Road Power Station; the two aspects of the Tube, the congregation of people and the raw power of the system, are subtly aligned. The film also emphasises the extent to which the Underground introduces itself into the mental and emotional life of its passengers. It becomes as much a protagonist as the characters themselves.

There is now a literature on the Underground, as well as of the Underground. 'Poems on the Underground', a project launched at Aldwych station in January 1986, has now been imitated by many cities and countries. The chosen lyric is placed in the carriages alongside the usual advertisements; it has often been confirmed that passengers will read and memorise the chosen poem as a memorial of their journey. The words of the poem are enshrined in the carriage and seem to float above the passengers' heads. So poets as diverse as William Blake and Lewis Carroll, William Shakespeare and Arthur Symons sing in concert beneath the ground. Ah sunflower . . . your hair is exceedingly white . . . Sometime too hot the eye of heaven shines . . . as a windmill turns in the wind on an empty sky.

I understand how the Underground can become an essential part of the personality. My dreams and memories have always been associated with the Central Line. I was brought up in East Acton, and educated at a school in Ealing Broadway. At various points of my early life I lived at Shepherd's Bush, Queensway and Notting Hill Gate. When I worked in an office I alighted from the train at Tottenham Court Road and then, at a later date, at Holborn or Chancery Lane. The Central Line was one of the boundaries or lines of my life. Now that I am beyond its reach, I feel free.

Yet, like the escaped prisoner yearning for his dungeon, I often dream of the Underground. I dream of lines going to improbable destinations all over the world. I dream of strange encounters on platforms with people I seem to know. I dream of coming up for air and being confronted by a transformed cityscape. I dream of running down passages in search of a platform. I dream of gliding down vast escalators. I dream of crossing the live rails from platform to platform. I dream of standing unsteadily in a carriage as it rattles along. And, yes, I dream of the Central Line.

11

Buried Secrets

The underworld is a place for secrets. It is a place of burial, of seclusion from the light of day. The notion of hidden treasure is a pervasive one. The London Silver Vaults are below the ground of Chancery Lane, and the Crown Jewels were until recently kept in a bunker beneath the Tower.

The temptation to bury precious objects is very strong, especially in times of danger. Criminal fraternities may bury their gains for many months before retrieving them. Jewels, coins, gold and silver plate, will still lie under the ground. If they could be unearthed, they would dazzle the city. A hoard of Roman gold coins, placed within a purse and then within a box, has been found in the City of London. During the Great Fire of 1666 Samuel Pepys buried his Parmesan cheese and wine in his London garden. His was an ancient instinct. The underworld, however, is not always safe. In the same conflagration the booksellers of St Paul's Churchyard put all their stock into the parish church of St Faith's, in the crypt of the cathedral, but the collapsed roof of the cathedral broke through. When the booksellers opened the vault the rush of air made the paper leap into flames and the books burned for a week.

The Jewel House in the Tower of London, 1841

Charles Dickens exhibited a proper London fascination for underground places when he declared in an essay, 'The City of the Absent' (1861), that 'the deserted wine-merchants' cellars are fine subjects for consideration; but the deserted money cellars of the bankers, and their plate cellars, and their jewel cellars, what subterranean regions of the Wonderful Lamp are these!'

The lamp still burns brightly. As the price of gold rises ever higher many London banks are building larger and deeper vaults to accommodate the precious metal; they are great caverns of treasure. It is estimated that 250 million ounces of gold are concealed beneath the ground. But no London cellar is more wonderful than the vaults of the Bank of England. They contain the second biggest hoard of gold bullion on the planet. A network of tunnels, radiating out from the bank, run beneath the City streets. Several thousand bars of 24-carat gold, each one weighing 28 pounds, are stored within them. They may be said to light up the bowels of the earth.

You would not know, on walking along High Holborn or Whitehall, that there is a secret world beneath your feet. There is no echo, no sign or token, of corridors and chambers below the surface. You would pass its gateways without giving them a second glance. Everything is contrived to seem as normal as possible. It is only when you understand the nature of underground London that you come to realise that everything is in fact something else. So the contagion of secrecy spreads.

In the centre of the capital, where the government agencies are situated, an underground world has been created. It is made up of tunnels, exchanges, bunkers, cubicles and larger command spaces. Many of them were

The arrival of the ingots, 1930

created in the period before and during the Second World War; others were constructed at the time of nuclear threat from the Soviet Union. Yet despite the passing of these immediate dangers, some of them are still in use for purpose or purposes unknown.

In 1939 a tunnel was constructed from the south side of Trafalgar Square to the Cenotaph, but this was only the first stage in what became a large underground network. The original tunnel was soon extended to what purported to be a telephone exchange in Craig's Court at the top of Whitehall; the exchange is still there, and remains almost completely unnoticed. The tunnels were then deepened and widened to take in Parliament Square, Great Smith Street, Pall Mall, Marsham Street, Horse-ferry Road, with an emergency exit in the basement of the old Westminster Hospital. It is an extensive network of underground life connected with the workings of the government.

A door can be found at the bottom of the Duke of York Steps that lead down from Carlton House Terrace into the Mall; a very large extractor fan is fastened to an adjacent wall. The door itself is barely visible. Another portal is to be found on the opposite side of the road, within the great ivy-covered bunker on the edge of Horse Guards Parade known as the Citadel. There were once four such 'citadels', the portals to subterranean London.

Of more open access are the Cabinet War Rooms buried beneath the Treasury. But other rooms and tunnels connected to it are not available for public inspection, for the simple reason that they are connected to the same complex beneath Whitehall.

The designers of the Cabinet War Room under Whitehall, L.C. Hollis and L.F. Burgis, in April 1946

In 1942 a vast and elaborate underground structure was built 100 feet beneath High Holborn, extending from Furnival Street and Chancery Lane to Red Lion Street in the north. It was designed to contain a deep bunker and a telephone exchange. An entrance can be found at 39 Furnival Street, and another at 31 High Holborn. They are both easy to miss, and are deliberately designed to be as unmemorable and as unobtrusive as possible. In Furnival Street are two black double doors that might lead to a warehouse; above them is a large iron pulley, for moving freight, and an air vent. Ventilation shafts are also visible in the adjacent Took's Court.

The portal at High Holborn is, at the moment of writing, covered by scaffolding. But if you peer through the glass doorway, you can see what looks to be a derelict lift. This is the lift that takes you eight floors down into the underworld. Two half-mile tunnels lie there, South Street and Second Avenue, as well as other tunnels constructed in the early 1950s. There is room for eighty people, with dining rooms and communal living areas as well as private cubicles. A six-month store of food was once kept here.

The Whitehall tunnels and the Holborn tunnels were then connected by a further tunnel beneath Covent Garden and extending south into Trafalgar Square. It comprised a miniature city beneath the surface. A journalist from the *New Statesman*, Duncan Campbell, penetrated this network of underground passages more than thirty years ago. He revealed that there were over thirty access shafts that 'connect these catacombs with the surface, most of them emerging unobtrusively in government buildings or telephone exchanges'. He found his own portal on a traffic island in Bethnal Green Road, as neglected and invisible an entrance as you could hope for. He descended 100 feet, complete with bicycle, and then began his ride under the ground. He described the air as 'fusty'.

He passed through the tunnel beneath St Martin-le-Grand, close to St Paul's Cathedral, and then journeyed west to Holborn by way of Fleet Street. He then went on to Whitehall, all the while guided by signs pointing to the various destinations. Among them were White-hall, the Mall, Leicester Square, Waterloo and Lord's Cricket Ground – all of them connected by a system of deep-level tunnels. He estimated the principal tunnel to be some 20 feet in width, with subsidiary tunnels of 9 feet. He found a red signal in one of them warning 'Danger'; this tunnel 'is unventilated and has no air in it'. But 'implausibly disguised as a touring cyclist I have often visited these tunnels'.

He re-emerged in the bowels of the Holborn Telephone Exchange. Campbell has published some photographs of his journey. The tunnels are eerie and somehow unsettling, like pictures of the deep ocean floor or the craters upon Mars. It was an astonishing journey, worthy to be recorded alongside other London pilgrimages. It can never be made again, however; after Campbell published the account of his escapade, in the *New Statesman* of 16 December 1980, all entrances to the system were carefully secured. This may be viewed as secrecy for the sake of secrecy, pointless and farcical, but it is testimony to the fascination that the underworld still exerts.

Other hidden passages run beneath Whitehall, some of them dug 200 feet below the surface. In one of them is situated the emergency strategy group known as COBRA. A newspaper report has described it as 'an air-pressurised network of low-ceilinged corridors leading to a large and dimly lit room'. Tunnels weave beneath New Oxford Street, and also in the area between the Strand and the Embankment. Various government departments of Westminster were placed in alignment, so that an underground refuge could be provided for hundreds or thousands of civil servants in the event of an attack; this was known as the 'black move'. A huge bunker is supposed to have been built beneath Parliament Square.

It is believed that a tunnel under the Thames joins the MI6 building at Vauxhall with the MI5 headquarters at Millbank; the Victoria Line between Pimlico and Vauxhall shadows its course. The Victoria Line does in fact pass beneath many notable buildings, and comes very close to Buckingham Palace. It has often been suggested that, at a time of grave national peril, it could be used to take senior ministers and members of the royal family out of London. A deep underground line was built to connect Elephant and Castle with Camberwell Green; it was supposed to be part of the Bakerloo Line, but in the 1950s its opening was 'deferred'. The tunnels still exist, but no trains run along them.

Wherever you look, underground London offers an echo or double image of the world above. Beneath the 7 acres of Lincoln's Inn Fields is an underground network that in 1939 was designed to harbour 1,300 people. There were, or are, underground trenches beneath Eaton Square, Vincent Square and Golden Square; refuges were also built beneath Hyde Park, Green Park and St James's Park. Smaller trench systems were constructed beneath eighteen other London landmarks, from Shepherd's Bush Common to the gardens of the Geffrye Museum in Shoreditch; they are now unknown and unseen. The tram subway running through Kingsway became for a while a subterranean flood-control centre kept away from the public gaze. It now lies empty and disused. But perhaps it is not altogether empty. One subterranean voyager, Michael Harrison, ended his account of secret tunnels in *London Beneath the Pavement* (1961) with a terse epigraph. He dedicated the book 'DIS MANIBUS'. To the gods of the underworld.

12

The War Below

At times of threat the world beneath the ground may
offer protection and security. It represents the age-old
instinct to return to the warm darkness that precedes
birth. The people of prehistory took refuge in caves,
reserving the innermost recesses for sacred activity. At
times of warfare in the twentieth century, when death
came from the sky, many Londoners sought instinctively
for safety beneath the earth.

In the First World War hundreds of thousands of
people went down into the Underground system in order
to escape the depredations of the Zeppelin airships. This
was unofficial activity, not supervised or controlled, and
no government shelters were ever provided. It was agreed
that people could take refuge on the platforms if an air
raid was actually under way, but not in anticipation of
an attack. In other circumstances a ticket was always
required before entrance was permitted. Some passengers
bought the cheapest ticket, and then continued around
and around the Circle Line until the likely danger had
passed. At the time of most danger, in February 1918,

the number of shelterers reached one-third of a million. There were some famous underground refugees. George V and the senior members of the royal family were, at the times of Zeppelin raids, taken into the tunnels near Buckingham Palace.

The experience of the First World War was enough to alert the authorities of a later conflict to the danger of a mass descent into the tunnels and platforms. It was assumed that the underground refugees in the Second World War would hinder the movement of trains carrying the dead away from central London to communal graves. More significantly, it was feared by officials from the Home Office and the Ministry of Health that Londoners might develop what was known as a 'deep shelter mentality' and refuse to come to the surface. It was believed, and stated, that the civilian population was likely to suffer 'a mass outbreak of hysterical neurosis' as a result of prolonged and intense bombing. Experts in the psychology of crowds suggested that 'people would regress to an earlier level of needs and desires'.

That 'earlier level' was of course enshrined in the Underground system itself, whereby people would descend into deep levels of the past. A spiritual, as well as chronological, dimension can be found in this flight beneath the earth. The citizens would become children again and 'would demand, with the all or nothing vehemence of infants, the security, food and warmth which the mother used to give in the past'. So many of them wished to return to the depths of Mother Earth.

At the beginning of the Second World War, therefore, London Transport displayed posters stating that 'Underground Stations Must Not Be Used As Air-Raid Shelters'. But who could thwart the primeval instinct of humankind? Three years before the outbreak of the war a film, entitled *Things to Come*, depicted hordes of anxious Londoners fleeing for safety from enemy attack into the bowels of the Underground. So the citizens in large part ignored the official warnings; they purchased cheap tickets, and then simply refused to come up again. In a complementary development some Londoners fled to adjacent caves in the tracks of their remote ancestors. The miles of Chislehurst Caves, dug over a period of 8,000 years, became the shelter for as many as 15,000 people. A hospital and a chapel, a cinema and a gymnasium, were built 70 feet under the ground just 10 miles from London.

The government had already taken its own precautions. Various government departments migrated underground. The empty passages and disused platforms of Down Street and Dover Street were pressed into service, while various rooms and passages connected with Hyde Park Corner, Knightsbridge and Holborn became part of the secret world of war management. The Tate Gallery stored much of its collection on disused Underground stations on the Piccadilly and Central Lines. The Elgin Marbles were lowered into an empty tunnel beneath Aldwych. A stretch of the Central Line, a 5-mile section of tunnel from Leytonstone to Gants Hill, was turned into an underground factory for the manufacture of spare parts for tanks.

In the first months of the war the raids on London were light and infrequent, but by the autumn of 1940 they became intense and sustained. In their panic the Londoners went under. They came with their children and bought tickets, costing 1½ pence, that gave them access to the underground platforms. If the first platform was overcrowded they boarded the train, and moved onto the next. Some people came in cars and motor coaches from the outlying boroughs, much to the resentment of the locals. The *Railway Gazette* reported that 'the vast majority of offenders are members of alien races or at least of alien extraction'. The truth of the claim is dubious, but it emphasises the extent to which an underground race might be considered to be 'alien'. The connotations of life beneath the surface were still injurious.

The people came with deckchairs, and rugs, and umbrellas; they brought quantities of food with them, some with as much as a fortnight's rations. They had come to stay. By six in the evening the passengers of the trains had to pick their way among recumbent bodies; two hours later, the platforms were so overcrowded that it was impossible to walk along them. The atmosphere became almost unbearable, and many people were forced to the surface for a few minutes to gulp the fresh air. A plague of mosquitoes, hatched in the unnatural warmth, caused further discomfort. When the electric current was switched off after the last train had passed, some shelterers squatted on the track. They also lay on the steps and the escalators.

Londoners sleeping on the escalators in 1940

When the sculptor Henry Moore descended into the Northern Line,

> I had never seen so many reclining figures and even the train tunnels seemed to be like the holes in my sculpture. And amid the grim tension, I noticed groups of strangers formed together in intimate groups and children asleep within feet of the passing trains . . . I never made any sketches in the Underground. It would have been like drawing in the hold of a slave ship.

It is an apt image of a vessel of slaves. In his drawings they become wraiths in the darkness, the pale cargo of humankind helpless in a world that has turned against them.

The government, and the officials of London Transport, soon understood that the situation was not going to be improved by inaction. Seventy-nine stations were designated as shelters for the civilian population; season tickets were issued for those using them regularly, and elementary measures of hygiene and sanitation were imposed. Wooden bunks were installed, to be replaced by metal versions when the wood became infested with vermin. It was determined that six people should occupy 6 feet of platform; three lay in bunks against the platform wall, while three others lay in front of them upon the platform itself. White lines were drawn, 8 feet and 4 feet from the edge of the platform, to designate sleeping areas. A special group of tunnel inspectors came into operation, and before long a refreshment service was introduced. Fifty-two lending libraries were established, and automatic cigarette machines were put in place. Some shelterers produced their own newspapers. The *Swiss Cottager*, for example, introduced itself to 'nightly companions, temporary cave-dwellers, sleeping companions, somnambulists, snorers, chatterers and all who inhabit the Swiss Cottage station of the Bakerloo Line from dusk to dawn'. In its second number it advised that 'vibration due to heavy gunfire or other causes will be felt much less if you do not lie with your head against the wall'.

It was perhaps what the authorities had feared, a world beneath the world. It was another city below the surface city. An underground race had been born. Yet it was still a fetid and noisome world, with the forced proximity of tens of thousands of people in barely habitable conditions. It resembled the rookeries of nineteenth-century London, and might have produced a population just as fearful and desperate. It also furnished an abiding image of the underworld as a place of filth and refuse.

There were casualties. When Trafalgar Square station

was bombed, seven people died. A similar incident at Bounds Green killed nineteen people. Balham station suffered a direct hit, killing sixty-four. One of the survivors recounted how he heard a massive roar overhead just before all the lights on the platforms went out. This was the nightmare of those living under the ground, with the return of primordial darkness. 'Then there was a smell of gas, and the children were shouting out for their gas masks. I got my torch and I flashed it up and saw water was pouring down in torrents.' He managed to open an emergency escape hatch. He still had the scars on his hands where people had been clawing at him. Other bombs penetrated the underground world. One train driver recalled that 'I seemed to have a sort of fear of the tunnel – of something coming through the tunnel.' A signalman at King's Cross recalled 'a terrible rush of wind. I stood over the levers and put my fingers in my ears. I remember feeling a rush of wind, and when I woke up I was lying down on the floor.'

So there were the familiar fears of fire and flooding associated with the underworld. The tunnels under the Thames were deemed to be most at risk; if a bomb pierced the tunnel and the water of the river came in, half of the entire Underground system would have been quickly deluged. From Shepherd's Bush to Liverpool Street, from Hammersmith to King's Cross, the water would have raged through the tunnels at an enormous velocity. So a sequence of twenty-five flood-gates was constructed, some of which still survive at the entrances of certain vulnerable tunnels. In the event only one tunnel beside the river suffered a direct hit. An old tunnel connecting Strand and Charing Cross stations was penetrated; 200 yards of its length were immediately filled with water but, fortunately, it had been sealed at both ends with concrete plugs.

Crypts and underground warehouses were also in use. Two huge subterranean facilities in the East End, 'Tilbury' under Commercial Road and 'Mickey's Shelter' under Stepney, became havens for the local population. Mickey's Shelter was named after a hunchbacked dwarf, by trade an optician, who organised the 10,000 people taking refuge with authority and resolution. He was one of the kings of the underworld. He had come forward in the face of the inaction of the government. The people had taken over the shelter and ran it for themselves. The administration had to all intents and purposes abandoned them.

In the autumn of 1940 the Tilbury shelter was described as 'a dim cavernous immensity' and as a 'vast dim, cathedral-like structure'. An observer reported that 'the floor was awash with urine. ... Some horses were still stabled there, and their mess mingled with that of the humans . . . The place was a hell-hole, it was an outrage that people had to live in these conditions.' This was the underground world to which the East Enders had fled. No heroism, or bravery, manifested itself; only misery and squalor. Henry Moore also visited Tilbury and in his notes recorded 'Dramatic, dismal lit, masses of reclining figures fading foreground. Chains hanging from old cranes.' This could have been the lower depths of the nineteenth century outlined in the engravings of Gustave Doré. Yet misery has no history.

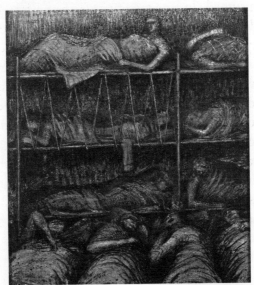

Henry Moore, *Shelter Scene: Bunks and Sleepers*, 1941

These conditions underground promoted political radicalism, as if an 'under-class' were truly ready to revolt. The *Swiss Cottager* denounced the government's 'indifference amounting almost to callousness, neglect, soulless contempt for elementary human decencies'. Partly as a result of public anger and concern, the government did begin the construction of eight deep-level shelters beneath existing underground stations, each of them able to hold 8,000 people; they were laid at a depth of approximately 90 feet. Half of them were converted to other uses as the war continued, but certain portals in the form of large Martello towers can still be seen on the surface as troglodytic monuments. That of Goodge Street stands on the corner of Chenies Street and Tottenham Court Road, while that of Stockwell has been converted into a war memorial. These portals could be knocked down, and the deep tunnels filled in, but what would be the purpose? Underground space has acquired the status of dark matter, unseen yet somehow maintaining the structure of the visible world. The portals are the gateways to immensity containing all that is hidden and all that is forgotten.

13

Deep Fantasies

Dreams and speculations are woven around the vistas of underground realms. They are regions of limitless possibility. A character in *The War of the Worlds* (1898) by H. G. Wells, in fear of the extraterrestrial invaders, states that

> You see, how I mean to live is underground. I've been thinking about the drains. Of course those who don't know drains think horrible things; but under this London are miles and miles – hundreds of miles – and a few days' rain and London empty will leave them sweet and clean. The main drains are big enough and airy enough for any one. Then there's cellars, vaults, stores, from which bolting passages may be made to the drains. And the railway tunnels and subways. Eh? You begin to see?

The fantasy of the underworld as a place of safety goes very deep. It is also an atavistic home. The female protagonist of Margaret Drabble's novel *The Middle Ground* (1980) cannot resist the odour of a street grating; she succumbs to the 'powerful odour of London' that allows her to 'escape the prison of the present into the past, where dark spirits swarm in the fast-moving flood'.

Other fantasies are of a more surreal cast. The tribes of Inner Mongolia believe that their country harbours portals to a giant tunnel that leads to a subterranean world dating from prehistory. The notion of a prehistoric world buried beneath the surface is compelling, and has excited the attention of many visionaries; Jules Verne's *A Journey to the Centre of the Earth* (1864) is one example.

Reports and speculations abound on the subject of an underground race. The narrator of Michael Moorcock's *Mother London* (1988) had once sought safety in the Underground system in the period of the Blitz, and since that time had become obsessed with 'lost tube lines'. These led him to fascinated speculation about the presence of an underground world beneath the surface of the city. 'I discovered evidence that London was interlaced with connecting tunnels, home of a troglodytic race that had gone underground at the time of the Great Fire. ... Others had hinted at a London under London in a variety of texts as far back as Chaucer.' Reports are common of 'lizard people', inhabiting caverns beneath the earth, and of the survivors from a sunken continent known as Lemuria. All is true in underground writing. Other narrators have told stories of tall beings that inhabit an underground world. They may be benign, meaning no harm to those above the surface, but there have also been tales of cannibals and other predators who attack those who live upon the outer earth.

The classic expression of this fantasy is to be found in Wells's *The Time Machine* (1895) when the narrator travels to the site of London some 800,000 years in the future. The Eloi live upon the surface in apparent bliss, but they are in fact being reared by a pale race of underground creatures known as the Morlocks; the Morlocks feed upon the Eloi, suggesting that the power and energy of the surface civilisation come from beneath in a world of mechanism. The underworld was a place where 'great shapes like big machines rose out of the dimness, and cast grotesque black shadows, in which dim spectral Morlocks sheltered from the glare. The place, by the by, was very stuffy and oppressive . . .' It seemed that 'Ages ago, thousands of generations ago, man had thrust his brother man out of the ease and the sunshine. And now that brother was coming back – changed!' Wells wrote his novel in the London of the early 1890s, at a time when the Underground system was in the throes of its expansion. So the narrator of *The Time Machine* remarks that 'there is a tendency to utilise the underground space for the less ornamental purposes of civilisation; there is the Metropolitan Railway in London, for instance, there are new electric railways, there are subways, there are underground workrooms and restaurants, and they increase and multiply'.

Legends and rumours concerning great kingdoms under the ground, with ancient tunnel systems leading to the upper world, are ubiquitous. Yet fantasies have an odd way of approximating or anticipating reality; if London continues to grow, taking up all available space, it may in some remote future be obliged as a last resort to go under the ground. Charles Knight, the mid-Victorian chronicler of London, was once moved to suggest that London might go the way of Babylon. He would envy the 'delight with which the antiquaries of that future time would hear of some discovery of a *London below the soil* still remaining'. That subterranean city exists even now.

The underground world also invites images of the sublime. The vastness of the space, a second earth, elicits sensations of wonder and of terror. It partakes of myth and dream in equal measure. 'The passion caused by the great and sublime in nature', Edmund Burke wrote, in his *Philosophical Enquiry into the Origin of Our Ideas of the Sublime and Beautiful* (1757), '. . . is astonishment; and astonishment is that state of the soul, in which all its motions are suspended, with some degree of horror.' He added that 'terror is in all cases whatsoever . . . the ruling principle of the sublime'. So we may view the underworld. The individual is unimportant in this subterranean world, a mere shadow on the wall – if, indeed, shadows can be seen in such darkness. There is a world, or worlds, within the world. Within the interior of the globe there may be a vast sea. There may be worlds where ancient creatures roam or where trees walk.

In Wells's *When the Sleeper Wakes* (1910) the narrator journeys through a subterranean world beneath London where there are 'fluctuating pictures of swathed halls, and crowded vaults seen through clouds of dust, of intricate machines, the racing threads of looms, the heavy beat of stamping machinery, the roar and rattle of belt and armature, of ill-lit subterranean aisles of sleeping places, illimitable vistas of pin-point lights'. This is a vista of immensity, taken up by many accounts of vast and elaborate underground civilisations with wild and delicate architecture, with a strange and suffused light, with marvellous perfumes and music. The underworld is a place of fantastic future cities, and Oswald Spengler believed that the cities of the future would indeed resemble great caves or caverns of stone. The fantasy only precedes the reality. In certain areas of London, where space is expensive, many owners of properties are already digging down and creating large subterranean spaces for a variety of uses. Some houses have been extended four storeys beneath the earth.

Francis Bacon once wrote that 'the truth of nature lies hid in certain deep mines and caves'. The mythic journey to the underworld was always undertaken in search of truth or the retrieval of lost beings; its purpose was to

'The People of the Future', a 1931 illustration to
H.G. Wells, *The Time Machine*

reveal what is hidden and to uncover secrets. It is no acci-
dent that in the nineteenth century, when the tunnels
and subways were first built under the earth, the sciences
of palaeontology and archaeology were effectively established. They were concerned with the things beneath.
They represented the search for ancient time or what has
become known as 'deep time'.

Before mines were dug in medieval Germany, a ritual

181

was held to propitiate the spirits of the earth. May this book be considered a votive offering to the gods who lie beneath London. We have completed, under their auspices, a long journey through the bowels of the London earth. We have come upon dreams and desires, fears and longings; there have been moments of wonder and moments of terror; the sacred and the profane have been found in close proximity. Dirt and squalor exist beside mystery and even beauty. It is the home of the devil and of holy water. The underworld moves the imagination to awe and to horror. It is in part a human world, made from the activities of many generations, but it is also primeval and inhuman. It repels clarity and thought. It may offer safety for some, but it does not offer solace. London is built upon darkness.

Bibliography

Ashton, John: *The Fleet: Its River, Prison and Marriages* (London, 1888)

Augé, Marc: *Un ethnologue dans le métro* (Paris, 1986)

Barton, Nicholas: *The Lost Rivers of London* (London, 1962)

Bell, W.G.: *Unknown London* (London, 1919)

Bradford, Tim: *The Groundwater Diaries* (London, 2004)

Brandon, David and Brooke, Alan: *Haunted London Underground* (Stroud, 2008)

Clayton, Anthony: *Subterranean City: Beneath the Streets of London* (London, 2000)

Daley, Robert: *The World Beneath the City* (New York, 1959)

Day, John R. and Reed, John: *The Story of London's Underground* (London, 1963)

Dobraszczyk, Paul: *Into the Belly of the Beast: Exploring London's Victorian Sewers* (London, 2009)

Douglas, Hugh: *The Underground Story* (London, 1963)

Duncan, Andrew: *Secret London* (London, 2000)

Emmerson, Andrew: *Discovering Subterranean London* (Oxford, 2009)

Follenfant, H.G.: *Reconstructing London's Underground* (London, 1974)

Foord, A.S.: *Springs, Streams and Spas of London* (London, 1910)

Gilbert, P.K. (editor): *Imagined Londons* (Albany, 2002)

Graves, Charles: *London Transport at War* (London, 1974)

Halliday, Stephen: *The Great Stink of London* (London, 1999)

—— *Underground to Everywhere* (London, 2001)

—— *Making the Metropolis: Creators of Victoria's London* (London, 2003)

Harrison, Michael: *London Beneath the Pavement* (London, 1961)

Haynes, Ian, Sheldon, Harvey and Hannigan, Leslie (editors): *London Under Ground: The Archaeology of a City* (Oxford, 2000)

Hill, Tobias: *Underground* (London, 1999)

Hollingshead, John: *Underground London* (London, 1862)

Howson, H.F.: *London's Underground* (London, 1981)

Jackson, Mick: *The Underground Man* (London, 1997)

Kelly, Michael: *London Lines: The Capital by Underground* (Edinburgh, 1996)

Kent, Peter: *Hidden Under the Ground* (Hove, 1998)

Lambert, G.W.: *The Geography of London's Ghosts* (London, 1960)

Lampe, David: *The Tunnel* (London, 1963)

Laurie, Peter: *Beneath the City Streets* (London, 1970)

Lawrence, David: *Underground Architecture* (London, 1994)

Bibliography

Legget, R.F.: *Cities and Geology* (New York, 1973)

Long, David: *The Little Book of the London Underground* (Stroud, 2009)

McCann, Bill (editor): *Fleet Valley Project: Interim Report of the Museum of London Archaeology Service* (London, 1993)

Newby, Eric, *A Traveller's Life* (London, 1982)

Pennick, Nigel: *Tunnels under London* (Cambridge, 1981)

—— *Bunkers under London* (Cambridge, 1988)

Pike, D.L.: *Subterranean Cities* (London, 2005)

Rolt, L.T.C.: *Brunel* (Stroud, 2006)

Ross, Christopher: *Tunnel Visions* (London, 2001)

Ross, Stewart: *History in Hiding* (London, 1991)

Sandström, G.E.: *The History of Tunnelling* (London, 1963)

Smith, Stephen: *Underground London: Travels Beneath the City Streets* (London, 2004)

Stevens, F.L.: *Under London* (London, 1939)

Sunderland, Septimus: *Old London's Spas, Baths, and Wells* (London, 1915)

Trench, Richard and Hillman, Ellis: *London Under London: A Subterranean Guide* (London, 1993)

Wolmar, Christian: *Down the Tube* (London, 2002)

List of Illustrations

Picture sources: Bridgeman Art Library 19, 79, 106, 109, 169, 181; British Museum, Crace Collection 39; Capital Transport Publishing 133; Nick Catford, 'Subterranea Britannica' 27; Gustave Doré, *London: A Pilgrimage*, 1872, 119; A.S. Foord, *Springs, Streams and Spas of London*, 1910, 89; Getty Images 160; Guildhall Library, City of London vi; Cecil Higgins Art Gallery, Bedford, Bedfordshire, UK / © Henry Moore Foundation / Bridgeman 174; F. H. Howson, *London's Underground*, 1951, 121; *Illustrated London News*, 15, 77, 102, 122; Charles Knight, *London*, 3v., 1841–4, 21, 55, 59, 86, 156; David Lawrence, *Underground Architecture*, 1994, 136; London Transport Museum Picture Library 140, 148; Henry Mayhew, *London Labour and the London Poor*, 2v., 1851, 6, 66, 72, 74; Museum of London 23, 50; G.R. Sims, *Living London*, 6v., 1933, 85, 96, 126, 131, 158; Thames Water 63, 91

Index

Index

Index

Index